CAPA for the FDA-Regulated Industry

Also available from ASQ Quality Press:

The FDA and Worldwide Quality System Requirements Guidebook for Medical Devices, Second Edition
Amiram Daniel and Ed Kimmelman

Development of FDA-Regulated Medical Products: Prescription Drugs, Biologics and Medical Devices
Elaine Whitmore

Safe and Sound Software: Creating an Efficient and Effective Quality System for Software Medical Device Organizations
Thomas H. Faris

Root Cause Analysis: Simplified Tools and Techniques, Second Edition
Bjørn Andersen and Tom Fagerhaug

Mastering and Managing the FDA Maze: Medical Device Overview
Gordon Harnack

Root Cause Analysis: The Core of Problem Solving and Corrective Action
Duke Okes

Get It Right: A Guide to Strategic Quality Systems
Ken Imler

The Internal Auditing Pocket Guide: Preparing, Performing, Reporting and Follow-up, Second Edition
J.P. Russell

Measurement Matters: How Effective Assessment Drives Business and Safety Performance
Brooks Carder and Patrick Ragan

Lean Kaizen: A Simplified Approach to Process Improvements
George Alukal and Anthony Manos

The Certified Manager of Quality/Organizational Excellence Handbook: Third Edition
Russell T. Westcott, editor

Enabling Excellence: The Seven Elements Essential to Achieving Competitive Advantage
Timothy A. Pine

To request a complimentary catalog of ASQ Quality Press publications, call 800-248-1946, or visit our Web site at http://www.asq.org/quality-press.

CAPA for the FDA-Regulated Industry

José Rodríguez-Pérez

ASQ Quality Press
Milwaukee, Wisconsin

American Society for Quality, Quality Press, Milwaukee, WI 53203
© 2011 by ASQ
All rights reserved. Published 2010.
Printed in the United States of America.

16   15   14   13   12   11   5   4   3   2

Library of Congress Cataloging-in-Publication Data

Rodríguez Pérez, José, 1961-
CAPA for the FDA-regulated industry / José Rodríguez Pérez.
    p. cm.
Includes bibliographical references and index.
ISBN 978-0-87389-797-6 (hardcover : alk. paper)
1. Pharmaceutical industry – Government policy – United States.
2. Food industry and trade – Government policy – United States.
3. Total quality management – United States. I. Title.
HD9666.6.R63 2010
615.1068′1–dc22
                                2010031139

Publisher: William A. Tony
Acquisitions Editor: Matt T. Meinholz
Project Editor: Paul O'Mara
Production Administrator: Randall Benson

ASQ Mission: The American Society for Quality advances individual, organizational,
and community excellence worldwide through learning, quality improvement,
and knowledge exchange.

Attention Bookstores, Wholesalers, Schools, and Corporations: ASQ Quality
Press books, video, audio, and software are available at quantity discounts with
bulk purchases for business, educational, or instructional use. For information,
please contact ASQ Quality Press at 800-248-1946, or write to ASQ Quality Press,
P.O. Box 3005, Milwaukee, WI 53201-3005.

To place orders or to request ASQ membership information, call 800-248-1946.
Visit our Web site at www.asq.org/quality-press.

∞ Printed on acid-free paper

Quality Press
600 N. Plankinton Avenue
Milwaukee, Wisconsin 53203
Call toll free 800-248-1946
Fax 414-272-1734
www.asq.org
http://www.asq.org/quality-press
http://standardsgroup.asq.org
E-mail: authors@asq.org

Dedication

This book is dedicated to my wife Norma and my son José Andrés. Their continuous support and love made this book possible.

Contents

List of Figures and Tables

Preface

Medical devices, biopharmaceutical, and traditional drug manufacturing companies devote an important part of their resources to dealing with incidents, investigations, and corrective and preventive actions. The corrective and preventive action system is known as the CAPA system. The CAPA system is second to none in terms of frequency and criticality of its deviations, and most of the regulatory actions taken by the FDA and foreign regulators are linked to inadequate CAPA systems. This guidance book provides useful and up-to-date information about this critical topic to thousands of engineers, scientists, and manufacturing and quality personnel across the life sciences industries.

Understanding the CAPA system is a fundamental prerequisite to improving it. Investigating and discovering the root cause of any event is just the starting point of the CAPA journey. After that, we must develop and implement adequate and effective corrective and/or preventive actions. A formal process must be established to evaluate how well implemented actions prevent the recurrence of those causes. Although preventive actions are half of the CAPA system, many companies do not have any true preventive actions. Understanding and improving the corrective and preventive actions system as a whole is the focal point of this book, the first of its kind dealing exclusively with this critical system within this highly regulated industry.

These pages evolved from hundreds of training sessions I have conducted as a consultant to dozens of regulated companies. By reviewing CAPA systems of nearly one hundred manufacturing plants (pharmaceuticals, medical devices, biological products, and food manufacturing), I developed firsthand awareness of the real issues of the CAPA system. These are addressed in this book in the form of a decalogue, a set of ten basic rules. Thus, the objective of this book is to help these industries improve their CAPA systems and succeed in their mission of producing safe and effective products.

Chapter 1 establishes the relationship between the CAPA system (identification, investigation, and fixing of problems) and the quality system environment. It also includes the most important definitions and concept of the CAPA world. I strongly recommend you begin by reading and understanding those critical concepts. Many people involved in developing and implementing corrective and preventive actions have trouble providing correct definitions of those concepts.

Chapter 2 describes the current requirements and regulations by type of products and by country (U.S., European Community) and by international harmonized documents. It also includes a review of ISO 13485:2003 requirements as they apply to medical device manufacturers as well as a review of the recent international guidance on CAPA for medical devices published September 2009. This chapter finishes with an overview of the current FDA regulatory trends related to the CAPA system.

Chapter 3 describes sequentially the entire CAPA process. It starts with problem detection, continues with root cause investigation, generation, and implementation of corrective and preventive actions, and ends with the evaluation of their effectiveness and the management of the CAPA system. Topics such as trending, evaluation of training effectiveness, and risk management concepts and their relation to CAPA are discussed in this chapter. Special emphasis is dedicated to the investigation of so-called "human error."

Chapter 4 contains useful hints to properly document the elements of the CAPA process.

Chapter 5 describes a decalogue containing the ten most common opportunities found in the CAPA system and how to fix them. Real examples are analyzed and best practices are discussed for each.

Chapter 6 presents the basic elements to be included as part of an internal CAPA expert certification, which is one of the recommended ways to reinforce your CAPA system.

Chapter 7 includes several forms that can be used as templates during failure investigations, development of corrective and preventive actions, and evaluations of effectiveness. These forms include dozens of questions that provide guidance and are a great help during the process of investigation and generation of effective actions to avoid the recurrence of unwanted situations. Also included is a form to be used when investigating human errors.

Finally, Chapter 8 presents a list of key recommendations to improve your CAPA system.

1
The Quality System and CAPA

1.1 THE QUALITY SYSTEM AND CAPA

A quality system is a set of formalized business practices that define management responsibilities for organizational structure, processes, procedures, and resources needed to fulfill product or service requirements, customer satisfaction, and continuous improvement. A quality management system (QMS) is a set of interrelated elements (processes) used to direct and control an organization with regard to quality. In other words, a quality system dictates how quality policies are implemented and quality objectives are achieved.

Continuous improvement is the result of ongoing activities to evaluate and enhance products, processes, and the entire quality system to increase effectiveness. The organization must continuously improve the effectiveness and efficacy of its QMS through the use of its quality policy, quality objectives, audit results, analysis of data, corrective and preventive actions, and the management review processes.

Analyzing data is an essential activity for any possible improvement at any level (system, process, and product/service). The organization must collect and analyze appropriate data to demonstrate the suitability and effectiveness of the QMS. This must include data generated as a result of monitoring and measurement and from other relevant sources. The analysis of data will provide information on customer satisfaction, conformity to product or service requirements, trends of processes and products including opportunities for preventive action, and suppliers.

Corrective action is one of the most important improvement activities. It identifies actions needed to correct the causes of identified problems. It seeks to eliminate permanently the causes of problems that have a negative impact on systems, processes, and products. Corrective action involves finding the causes of some specific problem and then putting in place the necessary actions to avoid a reoccurrence. Preventive actions are aimed at preventing the occurrence of potential problems. Correction of the problem is the third basic element of the corrective and preventive action system. These efforts attack symptoms rather than causes and sometimes are mentioned as immediate, remedial or containment actions.

The concept of CAPA is not restricted to any particular industry or sector. It is a widely accepted concept, basic to any quality management system. Since quality systems strive to continuously improve systems, processes, and products/services, there must be mechanisms in place to recognize existing or potential quality issues, take the appropriate steps necessary to investigate and resolve those issues, and, finally, make sure the same issues do not recur. Processes of the life sciences regulated industries (the manufacturing of medical devices, biopharmaceuticals, and traditional drugs) are plagued with deviations and nonconformities. Worldwide regulatory agencies perform thousands of inspections every year; often CAPA system violations are at the top of the list.

Within the United States, lack of adequate investigations, no true root cause analysis, lack of effective corrective actions, and lack of true preventive actions are common findings pointed out by Food and Drug Administration (FDA) inspectors. As evidenced by the significant number of problems related to this issue, companies are facing many challenges in making the CAPA system work as intended. Life sciences regulated companies must ensure that their CAPA system looks beyond product issues and considers other quality issues including problems associated with processes and systems. Unfortunately, a significant number of regulated companies are approaching the CAPA system very lightly, implementing corrections but no true corrective and preventive actions.

CAPA systems are inherently data driven. Without adequate, relevant data, it can be difficult to draw definitive conclusions about systems, processes, or product quality issues. One of the challenges many companies face is the proliferation of uncorrelated data repository systems within the organization. A typical example for U.S. companies is the existence of two separate systems (domestic and foreign) for investigating customer claims. Another example is the lack of relationship between supplier and internal CAPA systems. By having a correlated CAPA system, a company will be better able to diagnose the health of its quality system and will have a better chance of recognizing and resolving important quality issues.

As the quality system within an organization matures, there should be a natural shift in emphasis from corrective action to preventive action. Issues that must be corrected usually become obvious. However, issues that have the potential for becoming a problem are less readily recognized. How can a firm pore over its internal data to find those few situations that might be the precursors of problems down the road? The answer is part of the regulations. Companies must establish methods to evaluate both the *nonconformance* data (which will feed the corrective action portion of the system) and the *in-conformance* data (which will be the basis of preventive actions).

An effective CAPA system must be a *closed loop* system. This term refers to at least two elements of the CAPA system. First, it means there are sufficient controls in place to ensure that the CAPA process runs through all the required steps to completion, and that management and those responsible for quality have visibility and input to the process. In addition, top management must review the outputs of the CAPA system. Very often companies focus on completing the individual tasks of a particular corrective action, yet lose track of the original purpose of the CAPA system. For example, a particular product problem may be resolved, but no evaluation is ever performed to ensure that the solution was effective. In this example, the loop was never closed.

Second, a good CAPA system closes the loop on many of the documented issues by directly providing input into basic elements of the QMS such as design control. For example, nonconforming product procedures are directed at assuring that the nonconforming product is identified and corrected prior to distribution or prevented from being distributed. Frequently, a correction or temporary change will be implemented to assure that the affected material is fixed. An effective CAPA system will require that the problem be investigated and its root causes effectively attacked with the appropriate corrective actions.

A documented procedure for CAPA must define requirements for the following elements:

1. Collect and analyze quality data to identify existing and potential causes of nonconforming products or other quality problems.

2. Investigate the causes of existing and potential nonconformities.

3. Identify corrective and preventive actions.

4. Verify or validate corrective and preventive action prior to implementation.

5. Implement corrective and preventive actions.

6. Evaluate the effectiveness of corrective and preventive actions.

7. Ensure that the information related to quality problems or nonconforming products is disseminated to those directly responsible for assuring the quality of such product or the prevention of such problems.

8. Submit relevant information on identified quality problems, as well as corrective and preventive actions, for management review.

Finally, all CAPA system activities, and all quality system activities in general, must follow a risk-based approach. Because all existing and potential problems do not have the same importance and criticality, the prioritization of actions must correlate with the risk and the magnitude of each situation.

The four key CAPA definitions are:

- **CAPA (corrective and preventive action):** A systematic approach that includes actions needed to correct (correction), avoid recurrence (corrective action), and eliminate the cause of potential nonconforming product and other quality problems ("preventive action").

- **Correction:** Action to eliminate a detected nonconformity. Corrections typically are one-time fixes. A correction is an immediate solution such as repair or rework. Corrections are also known as remedial or containment action.

- **Corrective action:** Action to eliminate the causes of a detected nonconformity or other undesirable situation. The corrective action should eliminate the recurrence of the issue.

- **Preventive action:** Action to eliminate the cause of a potential nonconformity or other undesirable potential situation. Preventive action should prevent the occurrence of the potential issue.

1.2 CAPA RELATIONSHIP WITH OTHER QUALITY SUBSYSTEMS

The CAPA system is a critical component of an effective QMS and it must maintain a close relationship with other quality subsystems (as depicted in Figure 1.1). The ultimate goal of any regulated company must be to have a CAPA system that is compliant, effective, and efficient. All relevant subsystems that may produce nonconformances must be part of the process.

There are multiple feeders to the CAPA system, both internal and external to the company (as represented in Figure 1.2). Internal processes encompass both *nonconformance* and *in-conformance* results, internal audits and assessments, management reviews, and so on. External sources of CAPA process inputs are supplier audits and assessments, customer feedback, and results from external audits and assessment such as regulatory agencies, ISO, and so on. A detailed discussion of those feeders can be found in Chapter 3.1.1

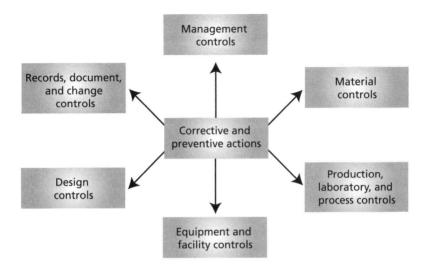

Figure 1.1 The CAPA system and the manufacturing quality system.

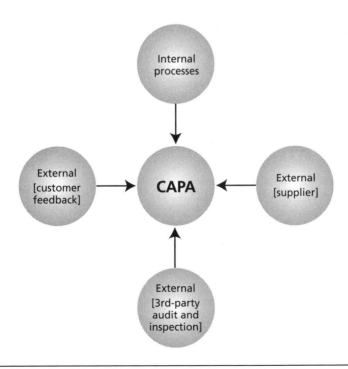

Figure 1.2 Feeders of the CAPA system.

1.3 CORRECTIVE OR PREVENTIVE?

One of the most sterile debates one can witness is the discussion between two CAPA professionals about whether a specific action they are working on should be considered corrective or preventive. The debate is pointless because what really matters is whether the action would attack a root cause.

To add even more confusion, one need only read the formal definition of corrective action. ANSI/ISO/ASQ Q9001-2008 section 8.5.2 defines corrective action as "action to eliminate the causes of nonconformities in order to *prevent* recurrence." ANSI/AAMI/ISO 13485-2003 contains the same definition, and the FDA regulation for medical devices (Title 21 CFR §820.100) establishes that each manufacturer shall identify "the action(s) needed to correct and *prevent* recurrence of nonconforming product and other quality problems." They use the word *prevent* as part of the *corrective action* definition.

To avoid any confusion, the word *prevent* is replaced by the word *eliminate* throughout this book; the definition of *corrective action* will read "action to eliminate the causes of a detected nonconformity or other undesirable situation. The corrective action should eliminate the recurrence of the issue."

A second common source of confusion and misunderstanding is deeper and more philosophical. Let's say that company A has a situation where root cause Z is creating a potentially dangerous upward trend, but the result is still within specification. Someone can argue that because the result is still *within conformance*, the action to be taken can be categorized as preventive. Others may perfectly well argue that it is a corrective action because the cause was already acting, even though the final result is still in conformance. My opinion is that it is a preventive action, but whatever you choose is fine; the important issue is to implement the action as soon as possible.

For the sake of clarification, Table 1.1 contains the rules followed in this book.

A typical situation that occurs during nonconformance investigations is the discovery of both existing and potential root causes simultaneously. In those cases, actions taken to eliminate the causes of nonconformance will be *corrective* actions, while actions taken against identified potential causes will be considered *preventive* actions. It is perfectly possible to have both categories of actions within the same CAPA plan.

Table 1.1 Corrective or preventive?

Situation	Examples
Name it *corrective action* only if you already have a product nonconformance or process noncompliance	• Product failing specifications • Confirmed customer complaint • Use of obsolete documents • Audit finding of product nonconformance or process noncompliance

Name it *preventive action* whenever the product, process, or system is still in conformance but you discover root causes with the potential to create nonconformities	• Developing adverse trends from a monitoring system (run chart or control chart)
	  – Shifts
	  – Trends
	  – High variability, and so on

Name it *preventive action* if it is purely a recommendation to enhance or improve any product, process, or system	• Changing to new material or new design • Implement new (enhanced) processes

A third controversy occurs when the same action can be considered both corrective and preventive when applied to different situations. Some CAPA professionals believe that once you have a corrective action (because you already had a nonconformance) to whatever product, process, or system you extend it, it will always be a corrective action. Other professionals, including myself, believe that if the same action can be extended to other products/processes/systems *not yet affected by this root cause,* then it should be considered a preventive action.

2

CAPA and the Life Sciences Regulated Industry

This chapter details those requirements for the CAPA system found in several U.S. and international life science regulations, as well as in the international standard ISO 13485:2003, which apply to medical device manufacturers.

In the United States, the main sources of CAPA regulations are the current good manufacturing practice (CGMP) for finished drugs (Title 21 CFR §210 & 211) and the medical devices QSR contained in Title 21 CFR §820. Several guidelines and guidances from the FDA will be reviewed in this chapter. It is important to note that U.S. FDA regulations are generally considered to be the most comprehensive of all medical product regulations; many non-U.S. regulations are derived from FDA requirements.

In the European Union (EU), pharmaceutical goods manufacturing practices are included in volume 4 of the *EudraLex* (the rules governing medicinal products in the EU). It contains guidance for the interpretation of the principles and guidelines of CGMP for medicinal products for human and veterinary use laid down in Commission Directive 91/356/EEC, as amended by Directive 2003/94/EC and 91/412/EEC respectively. In the case of medical devices, the market is divided into three areas for regulatory purposes: (a) Active Implantable Medical Devices Directive 90/385 EEC (AIMD), (b) Medical Device Directive 93/42 EEC (MDD), and (c) In Vitro Diagnostic Directive 79/98 EC (IVDD). These three directives must be considered a set because the AIMD was amended by the MDD and the IVDD amended the MDD.

---

[1] FDA guidance documents do not establish legally enforceable responsibilities. Instead, guidances describe the Agency's current thinking on a topic and should be viewed only as recommendations unless specific regulatory or statutory requirements are cited. The use of the word *should* in Agency guidances means that something is suggested or recommended, but not required. Author's comments: It's wise to follow the FDA current thinking.

Topics within this chapter are divided between U.S. and non-U.S. regulations. Within each, regulations are ordered by date of implementation. Following is an outline of this chapter's organization:

- FDA Pharmaceutical CGMP (Title 21 CFR §210 & 211), 1978

- FDA Medical Devices QSR (Title 21 CFR §820), 1996

- FDA Quality System Inspection Technique (QSIT), 1999

- FDA Investigation Out-of-specification (OOS) Guidance, 2006

- FDA Quality Systems Approach to Pharmaceutical Current Good Manufacturing Practice Regulations Guidance, 2006

- European Pharmaceutical GMP (*EudraLex* volume 4), 2003

- Harmonization Processes: ICH and GHTF

- ICH Q10 Pharmaceutical Quality System, 2008

- ISO 13485:2003 and the Non-U.S. Medical Devices Regulations

- Global Harmonization Task Force—Quality Management System—Medical Devices—Guidance on corrective action and preventive action and related QMS processes, 2009

- Current FDA Regulatory Trends for CAPA system

2.1 FDA PHARMACEUTICAL CGMP

The U.S. regulations governing drugs can be found in the *21 Code of Federal Regulations*. Parts 210 and 211 are named respectively *Current manufacturing practice in manufacturing, processing, packing, or holding of drugs* and *Current manufacturing practice for finished pharmaceuticals*. Originally issued in 1971, they experienced major revisions during 1978 and 1995. Sections related to investigation of unwanted situations can be found throughout the regulations. The CAPA acronym was first adopted by the FDA during the development of the medical device quality system regulations in the 1990s.

§211.22 Responsibilities of quality control unit.
There shall be a quality control unit...and the authority to review production records to assure that no errors have occurred or, if errors have occurred, that they have been fully investigated.

§211.100 Written procedures; deviations.
Written production and process control procedures shall be followed.... Any deviation from the written procedures shall be recorded and justified.

§211.192 Production record review

All drug product production and control records, including those for packaging and labeling, shall be reviewed and approved by the quality control unit to determine compliance with all established, approved written procedures before a batch is released or distributed. Any unexplained discrepancy (including a percentage of theoretical yield exceeding the maximum or minimum percentages established in master production and control records) or the failure of a batch or any of its components to meet any of its specifications shall be thoroughly investigated, whether or not the batch has already been distributed. The investigation shall extend to other batches of the same drug product and other drug products that may have been associated with the specific failure or discrepancy. A written record of the investigation shall be made and shall include the conclusions and follow-up.

United States v Barr Laboratories, Inc. 1993

This was a landmark decision because it provided legal strength to the concept "you can't test a product into compliance." It also established some requirements for failure investigation additional to those already included in CGMP. Among them:

- Specifies content of failure report
- Requires listing and evaluation of lots potentially affected
- Specifies that elements of "thoroughness" vary depending on nature and impact of the event
- Establishes that all investigations must be performed promptly, within thirty business days of the problem's occurrence, and recorded in written investigation or failure reports

2.2 FDA MEDICAL DEVICES QSR

The FDA published its *Medical Devices: Current Good Manufacturing Practice (CGMP) Final Rule: Quality System Regulations (QSR)* in October 1996 and it became effective June 1, 1997. This publication changed the focus of the regulatory agency to a "beyond compliance" approach. The various elements of the quality system (subsystems) are interconnected and interdependent. Companies must develop a systematic approach to their processes in order to be able to produce quality goods. Three main areas distinguish this new regulation from the typical GMP used for drugs:

- Design and development focus
- Purchasing control affecting suppliers, contractors, and consultants
- Corrective and preventive actions subsystem

Three subparts of the QSR are directly related to investigation and corrective and preventive actions:

- Subpart I §820.90 Nonconforming product
- Subpart J §820.100 Corrective and Preventive Action
- Subpart M §820.198 Records (Complaint files)

§820.90(a) Control of nonconforming product establishes that:
Each manufacturer shall establish and maintain procedures to control product that does not conform to specified requirements. The procedures shall address the identification, documentation, evaluation, segregation, and disposition of nonconforming product. The evaluation of nonconformance shall include a determination of the need for an investigation and notification of the persons or organizations responsible for the nonconformance. The evaluation and any investigation shall be documented.

The CAPA subsystem is described in Subpart J §820.100:

a. Each manufacturer shall establish and maintain procedures for implementing corrective and preventive action. The procedures shall include requirements for:

1. Analyzing processes, work operations, concessions, quality audit reports, quality records, service records, complaints, returned product, and other sources of quality data to identify existing and potential causes of nonconforming product, or other quality problems. Appropriate statistical methodology shall be employed where necessary to detect recurring quality problems;

2. Investigating the cause of nonconformities relating to product, processes, and the quality system;

3. Identifying the action(s) needed to correct and prevent recurrence of nonconforming product and other quality problems;

4. Verifying or validating the corrective and preventive action to ensure that such action is effective and does not adversely affect the finished device;

5. Implementing and recording changes in methods and procedures needed to correct and prevent identified quality problems;

6. Ensuring that information related to quality problems or nonconforming product is disseminated to those directly responsible for assuring the quality of such product or the prevention of such problems; and

   7. Submitting relevant information on identified quality problems, as well as corrective and preventive actions, for management review.

  b. All activities required under this section, and their results, shall be documented.

§820.198 describes the complaint files and establishes that:

  b. Each manufacturer shall review and evaluate all complaints to determine whether an investigation is necessary. When no investigation is made, the manufacturer shall maintain a record that includes the reason no investigation was made and the name of the individual responsible for the decision not to investigate.

  c. Any complaint involving the possible failure of a device, labeling, or packaging to meet any of its specifications shall be reviewed, evaluated, and investigated, unless such investigation has already been performed for a similar complaint and another investigation is not necessary.

  e. When an investigation is made under this section, a record of the investigation shall be maintained by the formally designated unit identified in paragraph (a) of this section. The record of investigation shall include:

   1. The name of the device;

   2. The date the complaint was received;

   3. Any device identification(s) and control number(s) used;

   4. The name, address, and phone number of the complainant;

   5. The nature and details of the complaint;

   6. The dates and results of the investigation;

   7. Any corrective action taken; and

   8. Any reply to the complainant.

2.3 FDA QUALITY SYSTEM INSPECTION TECHNIQUE (QSIT), 1999

Once the QSR were issued in 1996, the FDA created a team to re-engineer the inspection process used by the agency to perform quality system/good manufacturing practices inspections at medical device manufacturing facilities. The new inspection technique was called the Quality System Inspection Technique (QSIT). The QSIT approach to inspections was derived from the theory that there are seven sub-systems in the QSR (21 CFR, Part §820). Four primary areas were chosen to focus the inspection: management controls, design controls, corrective and preventive actions (CAPA), and production and process controls. The remaining three subsystems are covered via "linkages" within the QSIT guide.

Satellite programs are included in the QSIT inspection due to their correlation in the inspection process with the related subsystem. The CAPA subsystem is the logical "jumping-off" point to begin inspecting for medical device reporting, corrections and removals, and medical device tacking programs that relate to a firm's post-market activities.

Rather than check every aspect of the firm's quality system, the so-called "top-down" subsystem approach focuses on those elements that are most important in meeting the requirements of the quality system regulation and that are key quality indicators. Between 6 and 15 inspectional objectives are provided for the review of each subsystem. The review includes both a (broad) review of whether the firm has procedures in place and appears to meet the requirements, and a closer (detailed) review of some records to verify that the requirements have been implemented in actual production, design, and daily quality assurance situations. Without a doubt, this FDA document provides more details about the CAPA system. It also represents an extraordinary benchmark, advising companies where to align internal audit programs. The QSIT describes the CAPA subsystem as one of the most important quality system elements with an equally important purpose:

> To collect information, analyze information, identify and investigate product and quality problems, and take appropriate and effective corrective and/or preventive action to prevent their recurrence. Verifying or validating corrective and preventive actions, communicating corrective and preventive action activities to responsible people, providing relevant information for management review, and documenting these activities are essential in dealing effectively with product and quality problems, preventing their recurrence, and preventing or minimizing device failures.

I strongly recommend that anyone involved in CAPA read and fully understand the ten inspectional objectives. This is the most detailed information about the CAPA subsystem the FDA ever provided:

1. *Verify that CAPA system procedures that address the requirements of the quality system regulation have been defined and documented.*

Review the firm's corrective and preventive action procedure. If necessary, have management provide definitions and interpretation of words or terms such as "nonconforming product," "quality audit," "correction," "prevention," "timely," and others. It is important to gain a working knowledge of the firm's corrective and preventive action procedure before beginning the evaluation of this subsystem.

NOTE: Corrective action taken to address an existing product or quality problem should include action to correct the existing product nonconformity or quality problems and prevent[2] the recurrence of the problem.

The CAPA procedure should include procedures regarding how the firm will meet the requirements for all elements of the CAPA subsystem. All procedures should have been implemented. Once you have gained knowledge of the firm's corrective and preventive action procedure, begin with determining whether the firm has a system for the identification and input of quality data into the CAPA subsystem. Such data includes information regarding product and quality problems (and potential problems) that may require corrective and/or preventive action.

2. *Determine whether appropriate sources of product and quality problems have been identified. Confirm that data from these sources are analyzed to identify existing product and quality problems that may require corrective action.*

The firm should have methods and procedures to input product or quality problems into the CAPA subsystem. Product and quality problems should be analyzed to identify those that may require corrective action.

The firm should routinely analyze data regarding product and quality problems. This analysis should include data and information from all acceptance activities, complaints, service records, and returned product records. The firm must capture and analyze data from acceptance activities relating to component, in-process, and finished device testing. Information obtained subsequent to distribution should also be captured and analyzed. This includes complaints, service activities, and returned products as well as information relating to concessions (quality and nonconforming products), quality records, and other sources of quality data. Examples of other sources of quality data include quality audits, installation reports, lawsuits, and so on.

3. *Determine whether sources of product and quality information that show unfavorable trends have been identified. Confirm that data from these sources are analyzed to identify potential product and quality problems that may require preventive action.*

Determine whether the firm is identifying product and quality problems that may require a preventive action. This can be accomplished by reviewing historical records such as trending data, corrective actions, acceptance activities (component history records, process control records, finished device testing, and so on), and other quality system records

---

[2] Prevent is not a good choice to define corrective action.

for unfavorable trends. Review if preventive actions have been taken regarding unfavorable trends recognized from the analysis of product and quality information. Product and quality improvements and use of appropriate statistical process control techniques are evidence of compliance with the preventive action requirement.

Determine whether the firm is capturing and analyzing data regarding in-conformance product. Examples include capturing and analyzing component test results to detect shifts in test results that may indicate changes in vendor processes, component design, or acceptance procedures. Identification of these indicators may necessitate a vendor investigation as a preventive action. Monitoring in-process and finished device test results may reveal additional indicators of potential quality problems. For devices where stability is an issue, test results of reserve samples are continually monitored. These monitoring activities may trigger process changes, additional training activities, and other changes required to maintain the process within its tolerances and limits.

Determine whether the firm is using statistical control techniques for process controls where statistical techniques are applicable. An example would be "Statistical Process Control" (SPC). SPC is utilized to monitor a process and initiate process correction when a process is drifting toward a specification limit. Typically, SPC activities are encountered with large-volume production processes such as plastic molding and extrusion. Any continuing product improvements (in the absence of identified product problems such as nonconforming product) are also positive indicators of preventive actions.

4. *Challenge the quality data information system. Verify that the data received by the CAPA system are complete, accurate, and timely.*

Select one or two quality data sources. Determine whether the data are complete, accurate, and entered into the CAPA system in a timely manner.

5. *Verify that appropriate statistical methods are employed (where necessary) to detect recurring quality problems. Determine whether results of analyses are compared across different data sources to identify and develop the extent of product and quality problems.*

The analysis of product and quality problems should include appropriate statistical and non-statistical techniques. Statistical techniques include Pareto analysis, spreadsheets, and pie charts. Non-statistical techniques include quality review boards, quality review committees, and other methods.

The analysis of product and quality problems should also include the comparison of problems and trends across different data sources to establish a global view of a problem and not an isolated view. For example, problems noted in service records should be compared with similar problem trends noted in complaints and acceptance activity information.

The full extent of a problem must be captured before the probability of occurrence, risk analysis, and the proper course of corrective or preventive action can be determined.

6. *Determine whether failure investigation procedures are followed. Determine whether the degree to which a quality problem or nonconforming product is investigated is commensurate with the significance and risk of the nonconformity. Determine whether failure investigations are conducted to determine root cause (where possible). Verify that there is control for preventing distribution of nonconforming product.*

Review the firm's CAPA procedures for conducting failure investigations. Determine whether the procedures include provisions for identifying the failure modes and determining the significance of the failure modes (using tools such as risk analysis). What is the rationale for determining whether a failure analysis should be conducted as part of the investigation, and the depth of the failure analysis?

Discuss with the firm their rationale for determining whether a corrective or preventive action is necessary for an identified trend regarding product or quality problems. The decision process may be linked to the results of a risk analysis and essential device outputs.

Using the sampling tables, select failure investigation records regarding more than one failure mode (if possible) and determine whether the firm is following its failure investigation procedures.

Confirm that all of the failure modes from your selected sample of failure investigations have been captured within data summaries such as reports, pie charts, spreadsheets, Pareto charts, and so on.

Where possible, determine whether the depth of the investigation is sufficient (root cause) to determine the action necessary to correct the problem. Select one significant failure investigation that resulted in a corrective action and determine whether the root cause had been identified so that verification or validation of the corrective action could be accomplished.

Using the sampling tables, review a number of incomplete failure investigations for potential unresolved product nonconformances and potential distribution of nonconforming product. Unresolved problems that could be of significant risk to the patient or user may require product recall if the problem cannot be resolved.

Using the sampling tables, review records regarding nonconforming product where the firm concluded corrective or preventive action was not necessary. As noted above, verify that the firm is not continuing to distribute nonconforming product. This may be an important deficiency based on the class of, and the risk associated with, the product.

Using the sampling tables, review nonconforming product and quality concessions. Review controls for preventing distribution of nonconforming products. Product and quality concessions should be reviewed to verify that the concessions have been made appropriate to product risk and within the requirements of the quality system, not solely to fulfill marketing needs.

7. *Determine whether appropriate actions have been taken for significant product and quality problems identified from data sources.*

Where appropriate, this may include recall actions, changes in acceptance activities for components, in-process and finished devices, and so on.

Using the sampling tables, select and review significant corrective actions and determine whether the change or changes could have extended beyond the action taken. A significant action would be a product or process change to correct a reliability problem or to bring the product into conformance with product specifications. Discuss with the firm their rationale for not extending the action to include additional actions such as changes in component supplier, training, changes to acceptance activities, field action, or other applicable actions. Investigators should discuss and evaluate these issues but be careful not to say anything that could be construed as requesting a product recall.

8. *Determine whether corrective and preventive actions were effective and verified or validated prior to implementation. Confirm that corrective and preventive actions do not adversely affect the finished device.*

Using the selected sample of significant corrective and preventive actions, determine the effectiveness of these corrective or preventive actions. This can be accomplished by reviewing product and quality problem trend results. Determine whether there are any similar products or quality problems after the implementation of the corrective or preventive actions. Determine whether the firm has verified or validated the corrective or preventive actions to ensure that such actions are effective and do not adversely affect the finished device.

Corrective actions must be verified and (if applicable) validated. Corrective actions must include the application of design controls if appropriate.

Good engineering principles should include: establishment of a verification or validation protocol; verification of product output against documented product requirements and specifications; assurance that test instruments are maintained and calibrated; and assurance that test results are maintained, available, and readable.

9. *Verify that corrective and preventive actions for product and quality problems were implemented and documented.*

Using the sampling tables, select and review records of the most recent corrective or preventive actions (this sample may consist of or include records from the previously selected sample of significant corrective actions). To determine whether corrective and preventive actions for product and quality problems and changes have been documented and implemented, it may be necessary to view actual processes, equipment, facilities, or documentation.

10. *Determine whether information regarding nonconforming product and quality problems and corrective and preventive actions has been properly disseminated, including dissemination for management review.*

Determine that the relevant information regarding quality problems, as well as corrective and preventive actions, has been submitted for management review. This can be accomplished by determining which records in a recent CAPA event were submitted for management review. Review the raw data submitted for management review and not the actual results of a management review.

Review the CAPA (and other procedures if necessary) and confirm that there is a mechanism to disseminate relevant CAPA information to those individuals directly responsible for assuring product quality and the prevention of quality problems.

Review information related to product and quality problems that have been disseminated to those individuals directly responsible for assuring product quality and the prevention of quality problems. Using the sample of records from objective 9 above, confirm that information related to product and quality problems is disseminated to individuals directly responsible for assuring product quality and the prevention of quality problems.

2.4 FDA GUIDANCE: INVESTIGATING OUT-OF-SPECIFICATION (OOS) TEST RESULTS FOR PHARMACEUTICAL PRODUCTION, 2006

Originally published in 1998 as draft guidance, this guidance was finally published in 2006. It derived somewhat from the previously mentioned *Barr* case. Compared to the draft version, the steps of an OOS investigation are now described more clearly. In an effort to help pharmaceutical manufacturers evaluate test results, the FDA issued a new guidance on investigating out-of-specification (OOS) results that fall outside the acceptance criteria established in drug applications, drug master files, and official compendia or by the manufacturer. The designation also covers in-process laboratory tests. The guidance document covers such topics as:

- How to investigate OOS test results
- The laboratory phase of the investigations
- Responsibilities of analyst and supervisor and other laboratory personnel

- When to expand the investigation outside the laboratory to include the production process and raw materials
- Additional testing that may be necessary
- The final evaluation of all test results

Even though this guidance applies to chemistry-based laboratory testing of drugs regulated by the Center for Drug Evaluation and Research (CDER), it's one of the few FDA documents that make clear to regulated industries the expectation and interpretation of the FDA (the "how to do" things) regarding failure investigation. What may be one of its most important parts is found within the footnote on page six, which states:

> Please note that §211.192 requires a thorough investigation of any discrepancy, including documentation of conclusions and follow-up. Implicit in this requirement for investigation is the need to implement corrective and preventive actions. Corrective and preventive action is consistent with the FDA's requirements under 21 CFR part §820, Subpart J, pertaining to medical devices, as well as the 2004[3] draft guidance entitled *Quality Systems Approach to Pharmaceutical Current Good Manufacturing Practice Regulations,* which, when finalized, will represent the Agency's current thinking on this topic.

In other words, the FDA's expectation is that a CAPA system similar to the one included in the medical device regulation be implemented by all regulated industry.

OOS Guidance Phase I

Whenever laboratory error is identified, the firm should determine the source of that error and take corrective action to prevent recurrence. To ensure full compliance with the CGMP regulations, the manufacturer also should maintain adequate documentation of the corrective action.

Unfortunately, most of the laboratory failures are assigned to analyst errors (for example, due to a procedure not followed) and corrected by some kind of training intervention. For an in-depth analysis of this topic, refer to items #3 and #10 of the decalogue in Chapter 5.

OOS Guidance Full Scale Investigation

When the initial assessment does not determine that a laboratory error caused the OOS result and testing results appear to be accurate, a full-scale OOS investigation using a predefined procedure should be conducted. This investigation may consist of a production process review and/or additional laboratory work. The objective of such an

---

[3] This guidance was finally published September 2006.

investigation should be to identify the root cause of the OOS result and take appropriate corrective and preventive action. A full-scale investigation should include a review of production and sampling procedures and will often include additional laboratory testing. Such investigations should be given the highest priority. Among the elements of this phase is an evaluation of the impact of OOS results on already distributed batches.

A full-scale OOS investigation should consist of a timely, thorough, and well-documented review that includes the following information:

1. A clear statement of the reason for the investigation

2. A summary of the aspects of the manufacturing process that may have caused the problem

3. The results of a documentation review, with the assignment of actual or probable cause

4. The results of a review made to determine whether the problem has occurred previously

5. A description of corrective actions taken

If this part of the OOS investigation confirms the OOS result and is successful in identifying its root cause, the OOS investigation may be terminated and the product rejected. However, a failure investigation that extends to other batches or products that may have been associated with the specific failure must be completed (§211.192).

2.5 FDA GUIDANCE: QUALITY SYSTEMS APPROACH TO PHARMACEUTICAL CURRENT GOOD MANUFACTURING PRACTICE REGULATIONS, 2006

This guidance describes the aim of the FDA to bring the pharmaceutical GMPs to the level of the medical devices QSR. The introduction section of the guidance clearly establishes this purpose:

This guidance is intended to help manufacturers implementing modern quality systems and risk management approaches to meet the requirements of the Agency's current good manufacturing practice (CGMP) regulations (21 CFR Parts §210 and 211). The guidance describes a *comprehensive quality systems (QS) model*, highlighting the model's consistency with the regulatory requirements for manufacturing human and veterinary drugs, including biological drug products. The guidance also explains how manufacturers implementing such quality systems can be in full compliance with parts §210 and 211.

The guidance describes that CAPA is a well-known CGMP regulatory concept that focuses on investigating, understanding, and correcting discrepancies while attempting to prevent their recurrence. Quality system models discuss CAPA as three separate concepts, all of which are used in this guidance:

- Remedial corrections of an identified problem
- Root cause analysis with corrective action to help understand the cause of the deviation and potentially prevent recurrence of a similar problem
- Preventive action to avert recurrence of a similar potential problem

Under corrective action, the guidance establishes:

Corrective action is a reactive tool for system improvement to ensure that significant problems do not recur. Both quality systems and the CGMP regulations emphasize corrective actions. Quality systems approaches call for procedures to be developed and documented to ensure that the need for action is evaluated relevant to the possible consequences, the root cause of the problem is investigated, possible actions are determined, a selected action is taken within a defined timeframe, and the effectiveness of the action taken is evaluated. It is essential to document corrective actions taken (CGMP also requires this; see §211.192).

It is essential to determine what actions will reduce the likelihood of a problem recurring. Examples of sources that can be used to gather such information include the following:

- Nonconformance reports and rejections
- Returns
- Complaints
- Internal and external audits
- Data and risk assessment related to operations and quality system processes
- Management review decisions

For preventive actions:

Being proactive is an essential tool in quality systems management. Succession planning, training, capturing institutional knowledge, and planning for personnel, policy, and process changes are preventive actions that will help ensure that potential problems and root causes are identified, possible consequences assessed, and appropriate actions considered.

The selected preventive action should be evaluated and recorded, and the system should be monitored for the effectiveness of the action. Problems can be anticipated and their occurrence prevented by reviewing data and analyzing risks associated with operational and quality system processes, and by keeping abreast of changes in scientific developments and regulatory requirements.

2.6 EUROPEAN PHARMACEUTICAL GMP (*EUDRALEX* VOLUME 4), 2003

EudraLex is the collection of rules and regulations governing medicinal products in the European Union. Volume 4 contains guidance for the interpretation of the principles and guidelines of good manufacturing practices for medicinal products for human and veterinary use. There are several instances within directive 2003/94/EC referring to CAPA:

Article 10: Production
1. The different production operations shall be carried out in accordance with pre-established instructions and procedures and in accordance with good manufacturing practices. Adequate and sufficient resources shall be made available for the in process controls. All process deviations and product defects shall be documented and thoroughly investigated.

Article 14: Self-inspection
The manufacturer shall conduct repeated self-inspections as part of the quality assurance system in order to monitor the implementation and respect of good manufacturing practice and to propose any necessary corrective measures. Records shall be maintained of such self inspections and any corrective action subsequently taken.

EudraLex Volume 4, Chapter 1, Quality Management, Good Manufacturing Practice for Medicinal Products (GMP) revised 2008, refers to CAPA in three areas:

Good Manufacturing Practice for Medicinal Products (GMP)
vi. Records are made, manually and/or by recording instruments, during manufacture which demonstrate that all the steps required by the defined procedures and instructions were in fact taken and that the quantity and quality of the product was as expected. Any significant deviations are fully recorded and investigated.

Quality Control

    vi. Records are made of the results of inspections and that testing of materials, intermediate, bulk, and finished products is formally assessed against specification. Product assessment includes a review and evaluation of relevant production documentation and an assessment of deviations from specified procedures.

Product Quality Review

    iv. A review of all significant deviations or non-conformances, their related investigations, and the effectiveness of resultant corrective and preventive actions taken.

    viii. A review of all quality-related returns, complaints and recalls and the investigations performed at the time.

    ix. A review of adequacy of any other previous product process or equipment corrective actions.

The manufacturer and marketing authorization holder should evaluate the results of this review, where different, and an assessment made of whether corrective and preventive action or any revalidation should be undertaken. Reasons for such corrective actions should be documented. Agreed corrective and preventive actions should be completed in a timely and effective manner. There should be management procedures for the ongoing management and review of these actions and the effectiveness of these procedures verified during self-inspection. Quality reviews may be grouped by product type (for example, solid dosage forms, liquid dosage forms, sterile products, and so on) where scientifically justified.

2.7 HARMONIZATION PROCESSES: ICH AND GHTF

The International Conference on Harmonization of Technical Requirements for Registration of Pharmaceuticals for Human Use (ICH) brings together the regulatory authorities of Europe, Japan, and the United States and experts from the pharmaceutical industry in the three regions to discuss scientific and technical aspects of product registration. The purpose is to make recommendations on ways to achieve greater harmonization in the interpretation and application of technical guidelines and requirements for product registration in order to reduce or obviate the need to duplicate the testing carried out during the research and development of new medicines. The objective of such harmonization is a more economical use of human, animal, and material resources and the elimination of unnecessary delay in the global development and availability of new medicines at the same time as maintaining safeguards on quality, safety and efficacy, and regulatory obligations to protect public health.

The Global Harmonization Task Force (GHTF) is a voluntary group of representatives from national medical device regulatory authorities (such as the U.S. FDA) and the members of the medical device industry whose goal is the standardization of medical device regulation across the world. The representatives from its five founding members (the European Union, the United States, Canada, Japan, and Australia) are divided into three geographical areas: Europe, Asia-Pacific, and North America. Each of these actively regulates medical devices using its own unique regulatory framework. Founded in 1992, the GHTF was created in an effort to respond to the growing need for international harmonization in the regulation of medical devices.

2.8 ICH Q10: PHARMACEUTICAL QUALITY SYSTEM, 2008

The International Conference on Harmonization of Technical Requirements for Registration of Pharmaceuticals for Human Use (ICH) is a unique project that brings together the regulatory authorities of Europe, Japan, and the United States and experts from the pharmaceutical industry in the three regions to discuss scientific and technical aspects of product authorization. Their purpose is to make recommendations on ways to achieve greater harmonization in the interpretation and application of technical guidelines and requirements for product authorization.

The ICH Q10 document on pharmaceutical quality systems was adopted at step 4 of the process at the ICH steering committee meeting in June 2008. At step 4 the final draft was recommended for adoption to the regulatory bodies of the European Union, Japan, and United States. It describes the CAPA system as follows:

> The pharmaceutical company should have a system for implementing corrective actions and preventive actions resulting from the investigation of complaints, product rejections, non-conformances, recalls, deviations, audits, regulatory inspections and findings, and trends from process performance and product quality monitoring. A structured approach to the investigation process should be used with the objective of determining root cause. The level of effort and formality of the investigation should be commensurate with the level of risk. CAPA methodology should result in product and process improvements and enhanced product and process understanding.

2.9 ISO 13485:2003 AND NON-U.S. MEDICAL DEVICES REGULATIONS

Main non-U.S. regulations (European Community, Canada, and Japan) for medical devices are basically aligned (harmonized) with the

ISO 13485:2003 standard. ISO 13485: 2003 *Medical devices — Quality management systems — Requirements for regulatory purposes* has become the world standard for medical device quality systems and it was complemented by the publishing of ISO/TR 14969: 2004 *Medical devices — Quality management systems — Guidance on the application of ISO 13485: 2003.*

Canada has adopted ISO 13485:2003 as a Canadian national standard and labeled it CAN/CSA-ISO 13485:2003. In Europe it has been adopted as EN ISO 13485:2003. It is not mandatory to use EN ISO 13485: 2003 as the quality system standard, but any required system must be equivalent to this or better; even the low risk Class I devices benefit from a quality system that is in effect the core management system for a medical device company.

CAPA Requirements Within ISO 13485:2003

Sections 8.5 Improvement and 8.5.1 General require the organization to continuously improve the QMS. Such improvement can be implemented and maintained through the use of corrective and preventive processes, among others.

Under 8.5.2 Corrective action, the standard establishes that:

> The organization shall take action to eliminate the cause of nonconformities in order to prevent recurrence. Corrective actions shall be appropriate to the effects of the nonconformities encountered. A documented procedure shall be established to define requirements for
>
> a. Reviewing nonconformities (including customer complaints),
>
> b. Determining the causes of nonconformities,
>
> c. Evaluating the need for action to ensure that nonconformities do not recur,
>
> d. Determining and implementing action needed, including, if appropriate, updating documentation,
>
> e. Recording of the results of any investigation and of action taken, and
>
> f. Reviewing corrective action taken and its effectiveness.

Similarly, for 8.5.3 Preventive action:

> The organization shall determine action to eliminate the causes of potential nonconformities in order to prevent their occurrence. Preventive actions shall be appropriate to the effects of the potential problems. A documented procedure shall be established to define requirements for
>
> a. Determining potential nonconformities and their causes,
>
> b. Evaluating the need for action to prevent occurrence of nonconformities,

c. Determining and implementing action needed, and

d. Recording of the results of any investigations and of action taken, and reviewing preventive action taken and its effectiveness.

When comparing ISO 13485:2003 requirements with the content of the FDA QSR 21 CFR §820.100, the conclusion is that the intent of each document is consistent with the other in terms of the corrective and preventive action system. It can be concluded that the requirements established by the QSR are far more prescriptive.

Regarding control of nonconforming product, FDA's QSR provides more detail as to the items to be recorded in a nonconforming product situation. It explicitly addresses the need for an investigation in such a situation.

2.10 GHTF QUALITY MANAGEMENT SYSTEM—MEDICAL DEVICES—GUIDANCE ON CORRECTIVE ACTION AND PREVENTIVE ACTION AND RELATED QMS PROCESSES, 2009

In November 2009, the Study Group 3 of the GHTF released this proposed document for a five-month comments period. The scope of this document is to "provide guidance for establishing adequate processes for measurement, analysis, and improvement within the QMS as related to correction and/or corrective action for nonconformities or preventive action for potential nonconformities of systems, processes or products."

It also states that "the document is intended for medical device manufacturers and regulatory authorities. It is intended for educational purposes and is not intended to be used to assess or audit compliance with regulatory requirements. For this purpose the manufacturer will establish processes and define appropriate controls for measurement and analysis to identify nonconformities and potential nonconformities. The manufacturer should have established processes defining when and how corrections, corrective actions, or preventive actions should be undertaken. These actions should be commensurate with the significance or risk of the nonconformity or potential nonconformity."

Curiously, the task force decided that the acronym "CAPA" will not be used in the document because "the concept of corrective action and preventive action has been incorrectly interpreted to assume that a preventive action is required for every corrective action. This document will discuss the escalation process from different 'reactive' sources which will be corrective in nature and other "proactive" sources which will be preventive in nature. The manufacturer is required to account for both types of data sources whether they are of a corrective or preventive nature."

2.11 CURRENT FDA REGULATORY TRENDS FOR THE CAPA SYSTEM[4]

Figure 2.1 (drug and biotech products) and Figure 2.2 (medical devices) illustrate some noteworthy numbers for U.S. fiscal year 2009, which ended September 2009. Because medical devices regulation contains the CAPA subsystem, FDA statistics include CAPA as an individual item. Drug/biotech GMP does not include the term CAPA and for this reason this item cannot be individualized. However, always at the top of FDA drug inspection statistics is 21 CFR §211.192, under which most of the CAPA issues are included.

Table 2.1 (drug and biotech products) and Table 2.2 (medical devices) contain the comparison between fiscal years 2008 and 2009 for the top ten inspection observations.

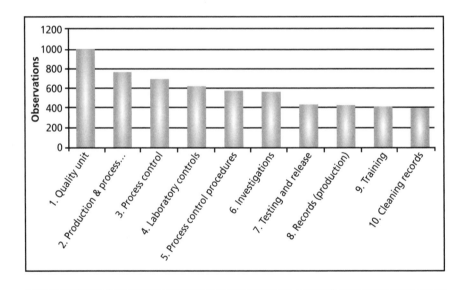

Figure 2.1   Top ten FDA observations during drug manufacturer inspections for fiscal year 2009.

[4] Presented by FDA at the Second Regulatory Conference of the American Society for Quality Puerto Rico Section held in San Juan, Puerto Rico, on October 23, 2009.

Table 2.1 Comparison of top ten observations during drug manufacturer inspections.

Top Ten Drug/Biotech Observations Fiscal Year 2009	Top Ten Drug/Biotech Observations Fiscal Year 2008
1. Quality unit	1. Quality unit
2. Production and process control procedures	2. Process controls
3. Process control	3. Laboratory controls
4. Laboratory controls	4. Investigations
5. Process control procedures	5. Production and process control procedures (not followed)
6. Investigations	6. Cleaning and maintenance of equipment
7. Testing and release	7. Production and process control procedures (not established)
8. Records (production)	8. Training
9. Training	9. Testing and release
10. Cleaning records	10. Records (production)

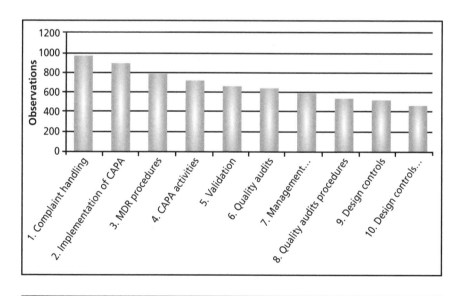

Figure 2.2 Top ten FDA observations during medical devices manufacturer inspections for fiscal year 2009.

Table 2.2 Comparison of top ten observations during medical devices manufacturer inspections.

Top Ten Medical Devices Observations Fiscal Year 2009	Top Ten Medical Devices Observations Fiscal Year 2008
1. Complaint handling	1. Complaint handling
2. Implementation of CAPA	2. CAPA procedures
3. MDR procedures	3. CAPA activities
4. CAPA activities	4. Validation
5. Validation	5. MDR procedures
6. Quality audits	6. Management responsibilities
7. Management responsibilities	7. Quality audits procedures
8. Quality audits procedures	8. Design control procedures
9. Design controls	9. Documents control procedures
10. Design controls procedures	10. Quality audits frequency

From 2002 to 2009, an average of 85 percent of medical device warning letters cited CAPA deficiencies.

3

Effective CAPA Process: From Problem Detection to Effectiveness Check

Τhis chapter describes sequentially the entire CAPA process. It begins with problem detection, continues with root cause investigation, generation, and implementation of corrective and preventive actions, and ends with the evaluation of their effectiveness and the management of the CAPA system. Topics such as trending, training effectiveness evaluation, and risk management concepts as they related to CAPA are discussed in this chapter. Special emphasis is dedicated to the investigation of the so-called "human error."

The basic CAPA process flow is shown in Figure 3.1 while Figure 3.2 describes the different stages and elements of the CAPA system.

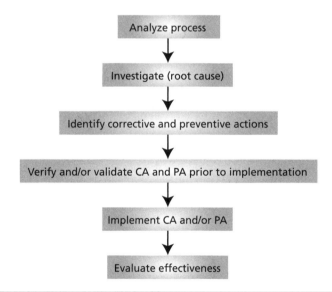

Figure 3.1 The CAPA process flow.

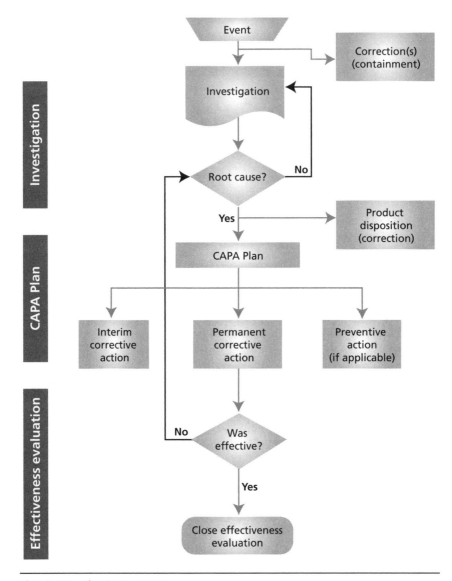

Figure 3.2 The CAPA system.

As easy as it seems, practically all manufacturers of medical regulated products are continuously struggling with their CAPA systems. The main areas of opportunity are depicted in the Figure 3.3, which represents the "vicious circle" of CAPA: lack of adequate root cause analysis leads to ineffective corrective actions, which in turn leads to recurrence of the issues, which leads to the need to investigate again and again the same old issue.

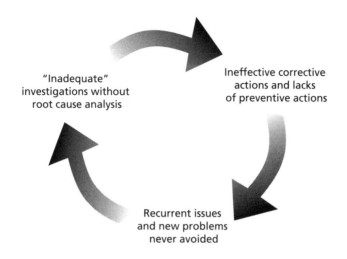

Figure 3.3 The ineffective CAPA circle.

3.1 PROBLEM DETECTION: DISCOVERING PROBLEMS

3.1.1 Source of Data About Product and Quality Issues

As previously mentioned, there is a perception in the life sciences industry that the CAPA requirements for U.S. medical devices are far more stringent than any other regulations established either by the FDA or by foreign regulators. Using this regulation as a guideline, there are three areas with requirements related to the identification of quality problems. Section 820.90(a), Control of nonconforming product, establishes that "as part of controlling nonconforming product, each manufacturer needs to evaluate each nonconformance, including a determination of the need for an investigation."

As part of the CAPA subsystem, §820.100(a) states that "each manu-facturer needs to analyzing processes, work operations, concessions, quality audit reports, quality records, service records, complaints, returned product, and other sources of quality data to identify existing and potential causes of nonconforming product, or other quality problems. Appropriate statistical methodology shall be employed where necessary to detect recurring quality problems."

Finally, §820.198 (complaint files) establishes that "each manufacturer shall review and evaluate all complaints to determine whether an inves-tigation is necessary." This section also clarifies that any complaint involving the possible failure of a device, labeling, or packaging to meet any of its specifications shall be reviewed, evaluated, and investigated, unless such investigation has already been performed for a similar complaint and another investigation is not necessary.

CAPA procedures must clearly identify what data sources are being used as input for the CAPA system. A frequent citation during inspections is that "the firm is not using all sources of quality data." Among the main sources we might consider:

- Acceptance activity records relating to incoming, in-process, and finished product testing
- Stability issues
- External (customer) complaints
- Internal complaints
- FDA 483s, warning letters, and published literature
- Corrective and preventive actions
- Reports of system, process, or product nonconformities
- Process monitoring data (for example, statistical control charts, trends, run charts, yields, and so on)
- Calibration and maintenance records
- Scrap, rework, "Use As Is," and other concessions
- Clinical adverse events
- Quality audit reports (internal, external, supplier, and third-party audits)
- Returned products analysis
- Training

In the case of medical devices, there are additional sources of quality data such as:

- Medical device reports and vigilance reports
- Installation and/or repair (servicing) reports
- Spare parts usage
- Customer and/or technical service requests
- Field service and/or warranty reports
- Customer feedback (for example, surveys)
- Historical records from previous corrections
- Lawsuits and other legal actions

3.1.2 Risk Assessment

Risk management concepts have been part of the medical devices world for many years. At first, the regulators used the term "hazard analysis" and it was part of the hazard analysis and critical control point (HACCP) methodology. For the last decade or so, HACCP terminology has been restricted to food safety and the FDA, ISO, and other regulators embraced the term "risk analysis," which evolved to the current broader term of "risk management." Risk analysis requirements are incorporated only into the design control (§820.30) element of FDA's QSR, but the preamble of this regulation includes mentions about risk analysis expectations across many elements. There is also an ISO standard (ISO 14971:2007), originally issued in 2000. This establishes the risk management requirements to determine the safety of a medical device by the manufacturer during the product life cycle.

For other regulated products, such as drugs, the application of the risk management concepts is very recent. It was done in the form of an international guidance document, ICH Q9 "Quality Risk Management," which was adopted as a non-binding guidance by the drug and biologic centers of the FDA in June 2006.

Having in mind those risk management principles, typical questions must be answered: *Do we always need an investigation? Do we always need corrective and preventive actions? How soon must companies fix their CAPA problems?*

CAPA and risk management are two interlocked concepts that cannot be separated. All of our decisions regarding CAPA must be filtered throughout the risk management system. Let's now answer these questions.

Regarding the first question: *Do we always need an investigation?* The theoretical response is yes. Every time we detect some kind of "problem" it is necessary to look into it. Repeating the primal concept of the CAPA system, continuous improvement requires the analysis of the issue to discover its root cause before we can implement actions to prevent its recurrence. To be able to fix the cause of the problem, we must first discover its causes. Without some kind of investigation or evaluation, the probability is low that we can reach the real root causes. However, resources are not unlimited (actually they are becoming more and more scarce) and definitively, not all issues have the same significance. As the QSR preamble states, "at times a very in depth investigation will be necessary, while at other times a simple investigation, followed by trend analysis or other appropriate tools, will be acceptable." Therefore we must prioritize and risk assessment is one of the best tools we can use for this purpose. The significance of the product or quality issue can be evaluated by considering the criteria described in Table 3.1.

Table 3.1 Risk assessment criteria.

Criterion	Categories and examples
Does it have the potential for a patient or user safety issue?	• **Critical or catastrophic:** can cause death or significant disability to a patient or user (contaminated injectable drug, critical drug mix-up, contaminated catheter) • **Marginal:** can cause minor injuries to patient or user (overpotent or subpotent drugs or incorrect diagnoses) • **Negligible:** no injury to patient or user (cosmetic defect, empty box without product)
What is the type or classification of the product?	• Device class I • Device class II • Device class III • Intravenous drug or sterile product • Drug other than intravenous (oral, cutaneous) • Drug with narrow therapeutic ranges
Does it affect the reliability, effectiveness or usability of the product? *Note: consider the worst case*	• Totally affected: not working, not usable, or not effective (missing product, broken device) • Partially affected: underfill, low count/quantity • Not affected
Does the issue cause the product to fall outside of established specifications?	• Final specification failure • Non-final specification failure • Acceptance specification • Validity (system suitability) specification
Does it affect the labeling of the product?	• Final label incorrect (lot number, expiration date) • Non-final label incorrect

Continued

Table 3.1 Risk assessment criteria. *Continued*

Criterion	Categories and examples
How frequent is the problem?	• First time occurrence • Occasional • Frequent
Has the frequency of the occurrence of the issue changed?	• Improving • Worsening
How difficult is it to detect the issue?	• No detectable (customer detected it) • Detected by chance (shipping operator detected it) • Detected by process (inspection detected the failure)
Does it represent a regulatory risk (can this product be considered as adulterated or misbranded)?	• Mix-ups • Product sold prior to completion of its record review

Most regulated companies perform some kind of risk evaluation based on the frequency and the severity (importance, significance) of the event. Situations in which the frequency is rare and the severity is low may not require further investigation. Nevertheless, this evaluation must be documented. In other words, if you can demonstrate (with objective evidence) that the problem has low frequency and no significant danger, then you could pass on this investigation and focus your effort on more significant issues.

The biggest concern with this evaluation is that a vast majority of regulated companies focused the severity evaluation exclusively on the safety of the patient. Based on that evaluation, they assigned very low risk scores to deviations and non-conformances that represent major violations of CGMPs and therefore render such products as adulterated.

Regarding second question: *Do we always need corrective and preventive actions?* If you investigated and discovered the root causes of the problem, it would be insane not to fix them. The FDA position in this matter can be found on the preamble to the October 7, 1996 Medical Devices QSR. In comment 159 of the preamble, which relates to the degree of corrective or preventive actions, FDA states "FDA cannot dictate in a regulation the degree of action that should be taken because each circumstance will be different, but FDA does expect the manufacturer to develop procedures for assessing the risk, the actions that need to be taken for different levels of risk, and how to correct or prevent the problem from recurring, depending on that risk assessment."

A remarkable observation on this side of the CAPA system is that many companies always require both corrective and preventive actions even in situations where no true preventive action can be applied. In some cases, the reason to require them is simply that the CAPA form includes both type of actions and therefore both are always required.

How soon must companies fix their CAPA problems? The third question refers to the timeliness of failure investigations and corrective or preventive actions. Timeframes for completing the different CAPA actions must be established based on the risk of the situation under investigation. In the fifth chapter, we will elaborate on this issue because it constitutes one of the biggest opportunities for improving CAPA systems. One simple approach used by several companies is to complete investigations (this is, the root cause investigation) in four weeks for low-risk situations, three weeks for medium-risk situations, and two weeks for high-risk situations. In the cases previously mentioned, risk classification is normally based on frequency and severity alone.

Our recommendation is to use risk management criteria to determine how deeply and how fast every nonconformance or deviation should be treated. These risk criteria must be clearly defined in written procedures. One example might be establishing who is responsible for evaluating product or quality issues and determining whether a failure investigation is necessary. Another example would be maintaining a record when no failure investigation is made, including the reason and the name of the individual responsible for the decision. The procedure should also determine the depth to which a failure investigation is to be carried out and when an investigation should not pursue corrective action.

Table 3.2 depicts a simple way to carry out this task by segregating nonconformances and deviations into three categories based on the previously described risk criteria. For each situation, an overall risk score is determined by considering the worst case scenario of the eight dimensions under analysis. Check marks indicate the risk classification that is assigned to each dimension. For example, if the problem can have a critical or catastrophic impact on the safety of the patient, then its risk score must be high independent of any other dimension such as product classification, problem detectability, and so on.

Table 3.2 can be applied to processes and systems including equipment failure where no product was directly affected.

Table 3.2 Risk assessment score matrix.

Criterion	Categories	RISK SCORE		
		Negligible or low (1)	Medium (2)	High (3)
Safety	Critical or catastrophic			✔
	Marginal		✔	
	Negligible	✔		
Product classification	Device class I	✔		
	Device class II	✔		
	Device class III		✔	
	Intravenous drug or sterile product		✔	
	Drug with narrow therapeutic ranges		✔	
	Other drug products	✔		
Reliability or effectiveness	Totally affected			✔
	Partially affected		✔	
	Not affected	✔		
Product specification	Final specification failure			✔
	Non-final specification failure		✔	
	Specifications are not affected	✔		
Product labeling	Final product labels			✔
	Non-final product labels		✔	
	No labeling is affected	✔		
Frequency or trending	First-time occurrence (Isolated event)	✔		
	Occasional but improving	✔		
	Occasional but worsening		✔	
	Frequent		✔	
Detectability	Not detectable or not detected			✔
	Detected by chance		✔	
	Detected by the regular process	✔		
Regulatory risk	Product can be considered as adulterated or misbranded			✔
	Product is not adulterated nor misbranded	✔		

Note: Drugs also include biopharmaceutical products.

Table 3.3 is an example of how to use this risk assessment score matrix for an issue affecting a medical device class III.

A medium risk score was determined for the example above. Now we can use this risk score to determine the content and priority level of each

Table 3.3 Example of risk assessment.

Criterion	Categories	Negligible or low (1)	Medium (2)	High (3)
		RISK SCORE		
Safety	Critical or catastrophic			✓
	Marginal		✓	
	Negligible	(✓)		
Product classification	Device class I	✓		
	Device class II	✓		
	Device class III		(✓)	
	Intravenous drug or sterile product		✓	
	Drug with narrow therapeutic ranges		✓	
	Other drug products	✓		
Reliability or effectiveness	Totally affected			✓
	Partially affected		✓	
	Not affected	(✓)		
Product specification	Final specification failure			✓
	Non-final specification failure		✓	
	Specifications are not affected	(✓)		
Product labeling	Final product labels			✓
	Non-final product labels		✓	
	No labeling is affected	(✓)		
Frequency or trending	First-time occurrence (Isolated event)	(✓)		
	Occasional but improving	✓		
	Occasional but worsening		✓	
	Frequent		✓	
Detectability	Not detectable or not detected			✓
	Detected by chance		✓	
	Detected by the regular process	(✓)		
Regulatory risk	Product can be considered as adulterated or misbranded			✓
	Product is not adulterated nor misbranded	(✓)		

nonconformance investigation (NCI) as detailed in the Figure 3.4. Table 3.4 describes the characteristics of each nonconformance investigation type.

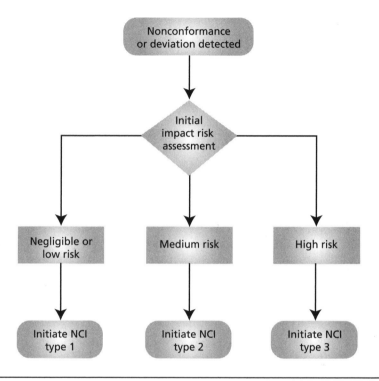

Figure 3.4   Risk prioritization of investigations.

Table 3.4   Type of nonconformance investigations.

Type 1	Type 2	Type 3
• Only negligible or low-risk scores are obtained	• At least one dimension had a medium-risk score	• At least one dimension had a high-risk score
• **One week** to complete	• **30 days** to complete	• **20 days** to complete
• Document the event and the corrections taken	• Document the event, root cause analysis, and the corrections taken	• Document the event, root cause analysis, and the corrections taken
• Monthly track and trending of type 1 NCI	• Need to generate a CAPA Plan	• Need to generate a CAPA Plan

Note: Complete NCI means document approval.

3.1.3 Initial Impact Assessment

A preliminary evaluation of the impact of the event based on the initial data and evidence available is one of the first actions to be taken once a problem is detected. It's important to establish, as soon as possible, the boundaries of the problem. If confidence exists that no other material has been affected, it must be supported with objective evidence. We need to consider product (lots/batches) directly affected by the event as well as any other product potentially affected. Special attention must be placed on products that ran before and after the lot under investigation. One of the most critical questions at this point is to establish whether any material affected by this situation reached the customer.

The preliminary investigation must determine whether any affected materials (in-process product, purchased or manufactured raw materials, or packaging components) have been processed beyond the area in which the situation was identified. If so, these other areas must be included as appropriate in the impact assessment.

Until the most probable root causes can be established, *everything is suspicious*. For example, once a product failed a specification:

- Other batches manufactured with the same components could be affected.

- Other batches manufactured/tested with the same equipment could be affected.

- Other batches manufactured/tested by the same operator/analyst could be affected.

Once the root cause is determined (for example, a component caused the failure), we can establish that:

- Other batches manufactured with the same components could be affected.

- Other batches manufactured/tested with the same equipment were not affected.

- Other batches manufactured/tested by the same operator/analyst were not affected.

The requirements for this impact assessment are clearly established in the CGMP (21 CFR §211.192):

> "The investigation shall extend to other batches of the same drug product and other drug products that may have been associated with the specific failure or discrepancy. A written record of the investigation shall be made and shall include the conclusions and follow up."

In the landmark judicial decision *United States v Barr Laboratories, Inc. 1993* there are requirements for listing and evaluating lots potentially affected by the failure under investigation. As a third example, the 2006 FDA guidance on investigation of out of specification establishes that:

> "Once the OOS is confirmed, the investigation changes from an OOS investigation into a batch failure investigation, which must be extended to other batches or products that may have been associated with the specific failure (§211.192)."

3.1.4 Process Trending

Process monitoring is a critical element of continuous improvement. Detection of nonconformances (for example, the failure of a specification) is not an issue in the life sciences regulated industry, and most of the time failure triggers an investigation within the CAPA system. The problem is the lack of monitoring for in-conformance processes. This is the kind of data that can allow us to identify potential causes of a nonconforming product or other quality problems. Many regulated companies are accustomed to monitoring environmental data, but they do not extend these concepts into the manufacturing or quality control test data. Without process monitoring, the control state expected from a quality management system cannot be achieved.

FDA regulations and guidances contain plenty of requirements and recommendations regarding trending of processes. For medical devices QSR says, under §820.100:

> "a. Each manufacturer shall establish and maintain procedures for implementing corrective and preventive action. The procedures shall include requirements for:
>
> 1. Analyzing processes, work operations, concessions, quality audit reports, quality records, service records, complaints, returned product, and other sources of quality data to identify existing and potential causes of nonconforming product, or other quality problems. Appropriate statistical methodology shall be employed where necessary to detect recurring quality problems."

For pharmaceutical manufacturing, the 2004 FDA Sterile Product Guidance states that "the QCU should provide routine oversight of near-term and long-term trends in environmental and personnel monitoring data." More recently, the landmark 2006 FDA Guidance for Industry Quality Systems Approach to Pharmaceutical Current Good Manufacturing Practice Regulations devoted a whole section to the topic titled *Analyze Data for Trends:*

> "Quality systems call for continually monitoring trends and improving systems. This can be achieved by monitoring data and information, identifying and resolving problems, and anticipating and preventing problems. Quality systems procedures involve collecting data from monitoring, measurement, complaint handling, or other activities, and tracking this data over time, as appropriate.

Analysis of data can provide indications that controls are losing effectiveness. The information generated will be essential to achieving problem resolution or problem prevention. Although the CGMP pharmaceutical regulations [§211.180(e)] require product review on at least an annual basis, a quality systems approach calls for trending on a more frequent basis as determined by risk. Trending enables the detection of potential problems as early as possible to plan corrective and preventive actions. Another important concept of modern quality systems is the use of trending to examine processes as a whole; this is consistent with the annual review approach. Trending analyses can help focus internal audits."

Trending relates to process behavior or process stability; process capability relates to the ability of the process to meet the customer specification. Process monitoring reveals the voice of the process. Statistical tools appropriate for this task include run charts, control charts, scatter diagrams, and regression analysis. However, it is important to remark that trending should not be confused with statistical significance. The use of appropriate terminology and wording helps in this task. When we obtain an out-of-specification finding (OOS), we call it a failure; however, when we obtain an out-of-trend finding (OOT), we call it an excursion.

Each company must develop a process monitoring/trending procedure where it must define what an adverse trend is. When an adverse trend is identified, an investigation should be initiated to identify the root cause(s) in order to implement effective corrective and preventive actions.

For environmental monitoring, both short- and long-term trending are used. At least three years of historical data must be kept for the purpose of long-term trending.

Short-term trending:

- Identifies potential drifts from historical results
- Amount required based on risk assessment of potential impact on manufactured products
- Provides daily and weekly excursion trend analysis
- Uses single sample point plots of all critical surfaces, areas, or utilities

Long-term trending:

- Used to document the state of control of environmental conditions; establishes normal ("natural") variability
- Helps to evaluate the effectiveness of: training, performance, cleaning methods, maintenance procedures, CAPA, and so on
- Used for weekly and monthly excursion trend analysis

The basic question when analyzing data for process trending purposes is this: *Do you see any trend or pattern that deserve further investigation?*

Several common mistakes occur during trending analysis:

- We conclude that there is a trend when what we are "detecting" is the common variation present in all processes.

- We are unable to detect a real trend or pattern (we're trend blind, a common problem in the regulated industry).

- We fail to evaluate enough data points to cover normal variation of the process under analysis. (At least 15–20 are required.)

Verify whether the most recent data points are within expected range of variation. Do you see any pattern? Any daily, weekly, monthly, or seasonal trend?

Are SPC or control charts the correct tool for process trending?

Most of the processes in the life sciences regulated industry are not stable over long periods of time. For example, the critical quality attributes of a drug are most likely determined by the incoming materials used during manufacturing. As soon as we change the raw material, we can observe dramatic changes in the results of quality control tests. For this reason, typical control charts are not the best option to monitor those processes. A good substitute is the run chart, which is basically a control chart without limits:

- Both have the same purpose: to distinguish common from special-cause variation in the data produced by a process.

- Run charts originated from control charts, which were initially designed by Walter Shewhart.

- Run charts evolved from the development of these control charts, but run charts focus more on time patterns while a control chart focuses more on acceptable limits of the process.

- Run charts are simple to construct and to analyze and can be used with any process and any type of data.

Nonconformance investigations type 1 (see Table 3.4) must be evaluated periodically using a Pareto chart to focus on the most prevalent issues. Other available tools such as run charts or control charts are recommended to monitor the performance of the most significant processes and activities such as rework.

I do recommend a monthly review of CAPA system trends. If, for some reason, this schedule is not feasible, review it bimonthly or quarterly. Less often than quarterly is not recommended.

Figure 3.5 is an example of monitoring of the scrap rate of a process. Baseline ranges from 2% to 3%, but something happened during December and the scrap rate rose to 7%. An investigation seems appropriate.

3.2 PROBLEM INVESTIGATION: DISCOVERING ROOT CAUSES

Many investigation reports conclude that the root cause was some kind of *human error* or procedures not followed (by some human being) and immediately we jump to solutions such as retraining. Most of the time these "solutions" are ineffective because they missed the core element of the CAPA system: root causes.

Problems are best solved by identifying and eliminating root causes, as opposed to merely addressing the immediately obvious symptoms. By directing corrective actions at root causes, we hope that the probability of problem recurrence will be minimized. Root cause analysis is one of the most widely used approaches to problem solving and it is considered an iterative process, part of the continuous improvement arsenal.

Many times the problems are consequences of a combination of causes or, even worse, of the interaction of these causes. For this reason, a systematic approach to root cause analysis and problem solving is highly recommended. The method and the tools to be used must be part of the investigation procedures. Making them requisites will ensure that your investigations are standardized enough and that they will enhance your overall CAPA system. Finally, but no less important, we should remember

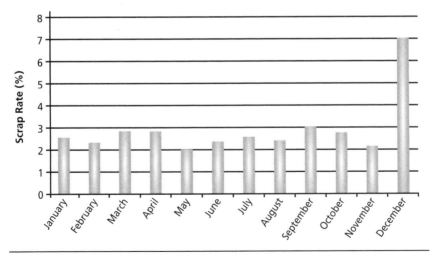

Figure 3.5 Scrap monthly rates.

that most of the time root causes are directly linked to some weakness of the quality management system.

3.2.1 Symptoms, Causal Factors, and Root Causes

When a company receives a customer complaint, or when a product fails its QC test, we are seeing only symptoms of some kind of problem. Problem symptoms and problem causes can look very much alike. For example, a broken piece of manufacturing equipment could be a symptom of poor maintenance, but it can also be the factor causing a product (manufactured with this equipment) to fail. This confusion between symptoms and true causes is especially dangerous in the case of the so-called human errors, which will be discussed later in this chapter.

The symptom can be defined as the obvious or detectable manifestation of a causal factor, the condition (human error, equipment failure, or material failure) that directly caused the problem, allowed it to occur, or allowed the consequences to be worse. On the other hand, root causes are the basic reasons why causal factors occur or persist.

The main tool used to dig in this problem-solving process is a series of questions. Asking what, where, when, and how will help to identify causal factors that contribute to the problem. Asking why will help us to identify the root causes behind these causal factors. Figure 3.6 illustrates this process.

Starting with a symptom or detected problem (all the products stored inside the walk-in cooler at the distribution center were damaged), we should ask why that occurred. The answer has two parts: First, products were damaged because the refrigerator ceased to work during the weekend; second, the alarm that should have alerted security guards about the incident did not work. Both are obvious causal factors, not root

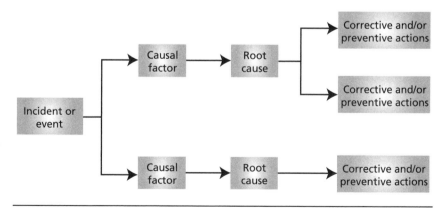

Figure 3.6 Root cause elements.

causes. Many times, there is more than a single factor behind our problem and we should pursue all of them if we want to avoid the recurrence of the situation.

Many companies will stop at this point and determine that the only "corrective action" needed is to fix the broken piece of equipment and the alarm system. Both are merely corrections because they aim at the symptoms and not the root causes.

Taking the first factor, we must ask why the refrigerator's motor broke. We might learn that its maintenance schedule is too long (one year) and some motor components deteriorated earlier.

We can continue by asking why someone wrote that maintenance must be performed only once a year and then we must shorten that period, which will be a good corrective action. We know that the root cause is found when we are able to fix it. Simply repairing the motor does not guarantee that it will not fail again if it is not effectively maintained at the required intervals.

For the second causal factor (alarm not working), the question should be this: Why didn't it work? We learn that it was properly installed but not included as part of the regular maintenance program. In this real case, no plant alarms were included in the scheduled maintenance. The fix to this root cause is also obvious: to include alarms in the maintenance procedure.

A classical technique regarding this topic is the use of the *5 Whys*. Must we always ask *why?* five times? The answer is no. Looking at Figure 3.6, we see that each *why?* will move us closer to the root causes. The first *why?* moved us from the symptoms to their direct causal factors. Sometimes the second *why?* finishes the work because it moves us to a fixable root cause. Other times, we must look at several layers of causal factors in order to discover the fixable root cause. The number of *whys?* is not a fixed factor; it will depend on the issue under investigation. Experience tells us that five is more than sufficient in many cases.

For the purpose of a simple investigation, the best use of resources might be to stop asking *why?* when you reach a "fixable" root cause. In this example, a couple of fine corrective actions could be to shorten the maintenance interval for all the refrigerator motors to a more logical interval (you will need to justify the new period), and to include all alarms in the maintenance program and procedure. The first corrective action can be extended as a preventive measure to other equipment having a long maintenance interval (first we must find them by performing a gap analysis of our maintenance program). The second preventive action should cover other equipment lacking maintenance in addition to the alarm.

Sometimes investigators try to fix world problems within a single investigation. Attempting to do so by continually asking *why?* will often focus an investigation on corporate procedures and policies. (How does this company establish maintenance schedules?) That could slow the process and prevent approval of the investigation report within a reasonable period of time. I firmly believe that it is more than adequate to fix those root causes under our control (the ones described above) as soon as possible and let management analyze and decide the next level of action. This is exactly the requirement established by FDA and ISO 9001:2008. In the refrigerator example (see Figure 3.7), the management of the plant will periodically review relevant CAPA issues (for example using a Pareto chart of root causes) and decide next steps. One decision could be to open a plant-wide or corporate CAPA to review the whole preventive maintenance program.

Table 3.5 shows several examples of symptoms, causal factors, and root causes.

Table 3.6 includes some examples of two typical causal factors often mentioned as root causes on investigations from FDA regulated industries.

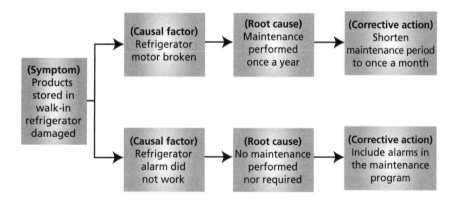

Figure 3.7 CAPA example.

Table 3.5 Symptoms, causal factors, and root causes.

Symptoms	Causal factors	Root cause
Fever	Infected wound	Poor hygiene
Bleeding of the gums that occurs regularly when brushing	Gum disease	Poor oral hygiene
Equipment broken	Inadequate maintenance or no maintenance at all	Procedure does not specify the maintenance or does not include it
Product not homogeneous	Operator did not follow the mixing procedure	Procedure is ambiguous and does not include sufficient details (e.g., mix for a few seconds)
Incorrect information entered into the manufacturing record	Operator did not follow the procedure	Operator not properly trained because of training environment
Mathematical calculation mistakes (for example, rounding errors)	Human error	Operators not properly trained on rounding numbers
Incorrect product label	Operators failed to detect the incorrect expiration date printed on the labels	Excessive load of work and an all-manual inspection activity

3.2.2 Problem Description

The familiar expression "a problem well defined is a problem half solved" perfectly explains the reason for this section of the book. Very often the main reason for faulty CAPAs is the attempt to fix the problem as soon as possible without first understanding and clearly defining it. During root cause analysis workshops, I frequently ask participants to forget about the solution (corrective and preventive actions) and focus instead on the full understanding of the issue we are trying to solve. Skipping this crucial step limits us to implementing only spot fixes that attack symptoms instead of taking adequate corrective or preventive actions aimed at root causes.

In other words, our problem-solving strategy must uncover root causes before we can determine the solution to the problem. We will use facts and data to narrow the search for the most probable root causes. We

Table 3.6 Examples of causal factors and root causes.

Causal factor	Potential root cause
Human error or procedure not followed	• Procedure not clear • Ambiguous or confusing instructions • Lack of sufficient details • Document format not adequate • Training instructor not adequate • Insufficient practice or hands-on experience • Frequency not adequate (insufficient refresher training) • Inattention to details • Lack of capabilities
Equipment failure	• Inadequate or defective design • Inadequate installation or validation • Historical lack of reliability • Equipment not included in the maintenance program • Inadequate corrective maintenance • Inadequate preventive maintenance

can conclude this introduction saying that if the problem is not clearly defined, completely and in detail, the problem cannot be solved!

I recommend the following four tools to describe/define the problem we are trying to solve:

- Flowchart—task analysis
- Chronology or timeline
- Change analysis
- Comparison matrix

Each tool includes references indicating where a detailed analysis can be found. My favorite single reference book for quality tools is *The Quality Toolbox* by Nancy R. Tague.

Flowchart[1]

A flowchart is a picture that describes the steps of a process in sequential order. It is useful when trying to understand how a process is really being done. Unfortunately, many companies do not have flowcharts of their processes. When trying to solve a problem, it is a good idea to spend some time walking through the process and comparing how things are actually done (the real process) with how they should be done (the theoretical process required by applicable working instructions). I especially recommend it when dealing with so-called human error; in this case, we can refer to it as a task analysis chart.

Chronology or Timeline

I recommend the use of a chronology or timeline. It can be defined as the arrangement of events in their order of occurrence. It must include a detailed description of events leading to the problem as well as those actions taken in reaction to the problem. Time is perhaps the most important element of any investigation because causal factors and root causes act on a specific and determined moment. Even if they seem to appear randomly, it is important to consider all pieces of information. The objective of this analysis is to determine when the problem began.

Ordering the facts of an investigation by time has two main purposes:

- It helps you understand the problem.
- It helps you write the investigation report.

During my workshops, I provide participants with case studies containing dozens of facts and dates. When completing the chronology analysis, most of them ignore at least half of those dates. Ordering the facts by time is often the only tool you need to discover the key path to the root cause. In the real example in Figure 3.8, it was noticed that the problem appeared (a sharp increase in the laboratory result variability) right after major maintenance work was performed in the facilities. Unsupervised maintenance workers moved calibrated balances and other laboratory equipment in order to perform their duties and then replaced them. The first and only apparent sign of these movements was that high variation.

Change Analysis

This tool helps to identify relevant changes in the process that may lead to the root cause of our problem. We can perform a change-point analysis to determine whether a change occurred, identify the moment of that change, and finally determine whether multiple changes have occurred. Most new (non-chronic) problems start with some kind of change, either new materials or components, new process, new people, or new specifications. The basic idea is to ask what may have changed prior to the detection of the problem.

---

[1] Okes (2009) and Tague (2005)

Date (week of)	Facts
October 12	Results within specifications
October 19	Floor maintenance housekeeping performed during the weekend
October 26	High variability of results. The two balances were found out of tolerance. Balances were calibrated.
November 2	Results within specifications
November 9	Results within specifications
November 16	Results within specifications
November 23	Results within specifications
November 30	Results within specifications
December 7	Results within specifications
December 14	Floor maintenance housekeeping performed during the weekend
December 21	High variability of results. The two balances were found out of tolerance. Balances were calibrated.
December 28	Results within specifications

Figure 3.8 Timeline of event.

In the example described in Figure 3.9, the graph clearly helps to identify that this company had two surges in customer complaints during the past year. The manufacturing dates of the faulty products align almost exactly with two situations where new operators were incorporated. Based on this information, the investigation focused on the evaluation of training received by these new hires. You can imagine the root cause.

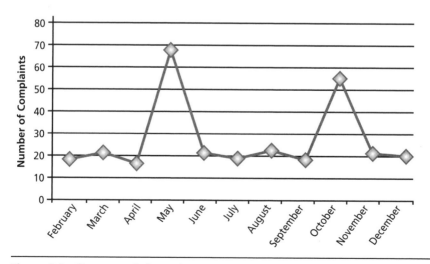

Figure 3.9 Change analysis graph.

Stratification or data segregation is a data analysis tool recommended when data from a variety of sources have been combined. In such a situation, it can be difficult to detect the meaning of the data. Data coming from several sources or conditions (such as shifts, machines, days of the week, or different suppliers) should be submitted to this analysis.

The stratification analysis can be performed graphically (scatter diagram, control chart, histogram, or other graphical analysis tool) by assigning different marks or colors to distinguish data from different sources. It can be statistically performed by using ANOVA. Data that are distinguished in this way are said to be "stratified." A typical use is to analyze productivity by machine to see whether we can identify any pattern.

Comparison Matrix[2]

The primary name of this tool is the Is–Is Not matrix. It is also called the K–T diagram in honor of problem-solving pioneers Dr. Charles Kepner and Dr. Benjamin Tregoe. It guides the search for causes of a problem or undesirable situation. By comparing *what, when, where,* and the *extent* of our problem (the *Is*) with *what else, where else, when else* and *to what other extent* the problem might have reasonably been (the *Is Not*), we can see what is distinctive about this problem and this leads us to potential root causes. The comparison matrix complements the change analysis tool previously discussed.

I prefer the use of the word *comparison* to name this tool because I have noticed many companies are using a variation of it that simply describes *what is* and *what is not* the problem without performing the critical comparison work, which is where the real value of this tool lays.

The final outcome of this comparison matrix is three paragraphs. The first describes our problem in detail. The second paragraph describes what *is not* our problem (but could have been). The third and most important paragraph describes the distinctions between each *Is* and *Is Not* pair (what is different, odd, special, or unusual about them).

The best way to use this tool is to hand it over to a cross-functional team. Typically the team encounters more difficulty trying to complete the *Is Not* column than the *Is* information. At times, due to the unique nature of some issues, the *Is Not* section cannot be completed for a specific characteristic. In this situation obviously no comparison can be made for such specific item of the matrix.

Very often, the information gathered at this stage of the problem-solving process is the base for the cause-and-effect diagram or the fault tree analysis tools describe in the next section. Once we arrive at the root cause, it can be tested against the comparison matrix facts to see how well it fits.

---

[2] Tague (2005)

3.2.3 Barrier Analysis[3]

Control barrier analysis is the evaluation of current process controls to determine whether all the current barriers pertaining to the problem you are investigating were present and effective. The origin of this concept relates to the safety field where the term "barrier" is used to mean any barrier, defense, or control that is in place to increase the safety of a system.

There are two main types of barrier, physical and administrative. Physical barriers are the most reliable in terms of providing failsafe solutions to problems. Administrative barriers are considered to be least reliable barriers, in terms of failsafe, because they rely on human action and behavior. Examples of each type of control barrier are included in the Table 3.7.

Table 3.8 depicts an example of a typical situation where a pharmaceutical product reached the market with incorrect information on its

Table 3.7 Barrier controls.

Physical barriers	Administrative barriers
• Separation among manufacturing or packaging lines • Emergency power supply • Dedicated equipment • Barcoding • Keypad controlling doors • Software that prevents further input if a field is not completed • Redundant designs	• Training and certifications • Clear procedures and policies • Adequate supervision • Adequate load of work • Use of checklist • Verification of critical task by a second person

Table 3.8 Barrier control analysis example.

Problem	Current controls	Current controls evaluation Why they failed?
Incorrect expiration date on label	Line clearance	Item not specifically included in the line clearance
	In-process manufacturing inspection	No formal checklist for inspection
	Final manufacturing inspection	No formal checklist for final manufacturing inspection
	Final quality product release	No formal checklist for final quality inspection

[3] Ammerman (1998)

label even though as many as four barrier controls were in place. Why did they fail? An egregious example of this situation was a product recently recalled because its label stated an expiration date of 07/2104 instead of 07/2014.

3.2.4 Root Cause Identification Processes and Tools

Once we have a well-defined problem with sufficient facts and data on the table, the next step will be the identification of all possible causes at the origin of the problem. Moving from the causal factors that directly created the symptoms to the true root causes very often requires the use of a disciplined approach including standard tools to identify root causes. It also benefits from creativity, good data collection, and objective and analytical reasoning.

Many of the chronic and persistent problems we face within the regulated industry are not the direct result of a single root cause. Many times, they result from a combination of causes or, even worse, from the interaction of causes. This is one of the basic reasons why the classic trial-and-error methodology of problem solving does not work most of the time.

It could be acceptable just to fix the problem if you are working in other less regulated environments. For the FDA-regulated field, we must effectively fix root causes, verify that the actions already taken have worked, and generate a documentation trail covering all the phases of the problem-solving exercise.

I have seen many regulated companies spend a lot of money on problem-solving training and still have a very poor CAPA system. While auditing their investigation and CAPA procedures, one can easily see the reason: a lot of *should be* and *can be* ("fishbone, fault tree, or any other problem-solving technique can be used") instead of *must be* ("fishbone must be included on every investigation").

The best recommendation I can provide to each company is to require (not simply recommend) the use of selected tools. I recommend the following four tools as requirements for any root cause investigation:

- Chronology
- Comparison matrix
- Cause-and-effect diagram
- Fault tree analysis

I have not seen a single case where the use of those quality tools has damaged the root cause analysis process. With some training, an average investigator can complete them in a reasonable period of time.

Cause-and-Effect Diagram

Cause-and-effect diagrams (Ishikawa diagram) are used to analyze and find the root cause of a certain effect or problem. These are also known as fishbone diagrams because the shape is similar to a fish skeleton. Fishbone diagrams are considered one of the seven basic tools of quality management.

The fishbone diagram focuses on the causes rather than the effect. Because there may be a number of causes for a particular problem, this tool helps us to identify the root cause of the problem in an uncomplicated manner. This tool allows brainstorming in a structured format similar to an affinity diagram, where potential causes are grouped into logical categories such as materials, manpower, methods, machines, environment, and so on.

Potential causes can be further tracked back to the root cause using the *5 Whys* technique. Another way to do this is to examine the problem using typical categories known as the 5 Ms and 1 E:

- Manpower: Anyone involved with the process

- Methods: How the process is performed and the specific requirements for doing it, such as policies, procedures, instructions, and regulations

- Machines: Any equipment, computers, or tools required to accomplish the task

- Materials: Raw materials, parts, and components used to produce the final product

- Measurements: Data generated from the process that are used to evaluate it

- Environment: Environmental conditions such as humidity and temperature and the culture in which the process operates

In addition to using the fishbone diagram (or a table containing the categories and potential causes), it is recommended to include a detailed discussion of each category as part of your investigation report. Do not simply document the most probable cause based on your analysis. You must always include in your discussion the reason why you discarded most of the identified potential causes and what objective evidence you have to support your selection of the root cause or most probable root cause.

Fault Tree Analysis[4]

Fault tree analysis (FTA) is a type of analysis in which a failure is analyzed using Boolean logic to combine a series of lower-level events (causal factors) until we reach their root causes. This analysis method was originally developed to quantitatively determine the probability of a safety hazard in the field of safety engineering.

---

[4] Tague (2005)

Fault tree analysis provides a method of breaking down chains of failures. A key addition permits the identification of combinations or interactions of events that cause other failure events. There are two types of interaction:

1. Several items must fail together to cause another item to fail ("AND" combination)

2. Only one of a number of possible events must happen to cause another item to fail ("OR" combination)

The "AND" and "OR" are called *gates*. They prevent the failure event above them to occur unless their specific conditions are met. When several factors must happen simultaneously ("AND" relationship), we can avoid the failure simply by controlling one of them (the easiest or the cheapest). (See the fire example in Figure 3.10.) When any of several causal factors can create the failure, then we must fix all of them.

The tree is constructed working backward from a known event or failure and asking why it happened. The answer will represent the factor that directly caused the failure. Continuing with the *why* questioning will allow us to reach fundamental events or root causes. In other words, the FTA is a very good tool to help us understand how an event occurred. It is best used when working with complex issues with several interrelated causes of failure.

FTA is a deductive, top-down approach to failure mode analysis aimed at analyzing the possible causes of an undesired event or failure. This contrasts with failure modes and effects analysis (FMEA), an inductive, bottom-up analysis method aimed at analyzing the effects of single-component or function failures on equipment or systems.

In terms of the CAPA system, we can define FTA as a reactive investigation tool (the failure already happened). FMEA should, ideally, be used proactively (during the design phase of a process) to anticipate failure modes and generate preventive actions.

For a detailed description and examples of this tool, see Tague (2005).

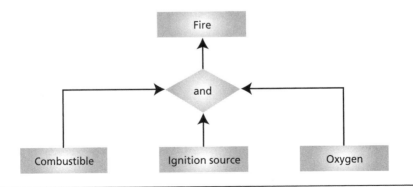

Figure 3.10 Fault tree analysis example.

A Few Words About the 5 Whys

One of the most repeated words in the past few pages is *why*. As an investigator, you are searching for the true causes of your problems. If you don't know the cause, you cannot implement corrective action. Remember the definition of corrective action: action to avoid the recurrence of root causes. There are plenty of root cause analysis tools available to you, most of them more complicated to understand than your own problem, but all of them are based on the word *why*.

The best way to find your way from the symptoms to the root causes is to ask *why* until the nature of your problem and its solution become clear. This tool (the 5 *Whys*) is attributed to one of the founders of the Toyota Company (Sakichi Toyoda).

Why five? It is postulated that five iterations is generally sufficient to get to a root cause. My recommendation is that you keep asking *why* until a fixable root cause is found.

Once You Have Found the Root Cause or Causes of Your Problem

Another possible outcome of the root cause investigation is that sometimes you will arrive nowhere. If you cannot find the root cause, you will be unable to develop corrective action. In this situation you must be sure to generate a complete investigation report demonstrating the problem-solving work performed. Any educated reviewer of your report must be able to conclude that your inability to find the root cause was not the result of a poor investigation. Be sure to look for potential root causes that you can attack through preventive actions. After all, without corrective actions, those preventive actions are all you can do to improve your process.

If you perform a methodical investigation, most of the time you will discover fixable root causes related to the situation you are working on. When several causes are identified, all of them must be addressed within the CAPA plan. Failing to do that is one of the biggest opportunities of the CAPA system as discussed in Chapter 5.

The trending of root cause categories is one of the most critical metrics management must periodically evaluate. To help with this process, I offer a list including almost 60 categories I have been developing for years. It can help to reinforce your CAPA system in several ways:

- Increases consistency across all investigations
- Facilitates consistency across the organization
- Allows trending of categories and root causes

The root cause list *is not* meant to be used for picking a cause without the proper root cause analysis process. This list is not static and can be modified to include new categories. However, resist the temptation to create an "other" category. You are likely to finish with most of the root causes classified as "other" and this defeats the purpose of the list.

Once you arrive at the root cause, try to confirm it. If possible and practical, conduct a controlled experiment to verify that the root cause effectively creates the symptoms you detected.

3.2.5 Root Cause Categories

1. **Personal Performance**
   1.1 Lack of attention (inattention to details, working from memory)
   1.2 Continuous attitude problems
   1.3 Fatigue
   1.4 Lack of capability (sensory, physical, intellectual)
   1.5 Personal problems
   1.6 Medication problems

2. **Training**
   2.1 Lack of training
      2.1.1 Training not required
      2.1.2 Missing training
   2.2 Training not effective
      2.2.1 Content not adequate (task analysis, qualification/certification)
      2.2.2 Training method not adequate
      2.2.3 Language barriers
      2.2.4 Environment not adequate
      2.2.5 Instructor not adequate
      2.2.6 Insufficient practice or hands-on experience
      2.2.7 Frequency not adequate (insufficient refresher training)

3. **Equipment**
   3.1 Design and/or installation
      3.1.1 Inadequate or defective design
      3.1.2 Inadequate installation or validation
   3.2 Equipment reliability
      3.2.1 Historical lack of reliability
   3.3 Equipment maintenance
      3.3.1 Equipment not included in the maintenance program
      3.3.2 Inadequate corrective maintenance
      3.3.3 Inadequate preventive maintenance
   3.4 Calibration issues
      3.4.1 Equipment not calibrated
      3.4.2 Missing equipment
   3.5 Utilization of the equipment
      3.5.1 Incorrect utilization of the equipment

4. Human Reliability Factors
  4.1 Work area
    4.1.1 Inadequate location of equipment
    4.1.2 Inadequate identification of equipment, materials, etc
    4.1.3 Cluttered or inadequate layout
  4.2 Work environment
    4.2.1 Uncomfortable environment conditions (cold, hot, poor illumination)
    4.2.2 Inadequate housekeeping
    4.2.3 Stress conditions (rush)
  4.3 Work load
    4.3.1 Excessive work load
    4.3.2 Excessive calculation or data manipulation

5. Procedures and Instructions
  5.1 Not used
    5.1.1 Lack of procedure or instruction
    5.1.2 Not required
    5.1.3 Not available or difficult to obtain
    5.1.4 Difficult to use
  5.2 Misleading or confusing
    5.2.1 Ambiguous or confusing instructions
    5.2.2 Lack of sufficient details
    5.2.3 Document format not adequate
  5.3 Wrong or incomplete
    5.3.1 Incomplete instructions
    5.3.2 Wrong instruction
    5.3.3 Typographical error
  5.4 Obsolete
    5.4.1 Obsolete document

6. Materials
  6.1 Material controls
    6.1.1 Inadequate storage conditions
    6.1.2 Inadequate sampling
    6.1.3 Material not adequate (hold, quarantined)
    6.1.4 Inadequate material substitution
    6.1.5 Shipping damage
    6.1.6 Marginal material
  6.2 Purchasing control
    6.2.1 Specification not appropriate
    6.2.2 Marginal supplier
    6.2.3 Supplier not approved

7. **Environment**
   7.1 Inadequate pest control
   7.2 Unfavorable ambient conditions

8. **Supervision and Management Factors**
   8.1 Verbal instructions/communication problem
   8.2 Inadequate communication between shifts
   8.3 Inadequate supervision
   8.4 Improper resources allocation (lack of personnel)

3.2.6 Investigating Human Errors

For many years we considered human errors or mistakes the cause of a mishap or problem. Human error, under whatever label (procedures not followed, lack of attention, or simply human error), was the conclusion of the investigation. Very often it was coupled with some kind of training activity (most frequently re-training) as corrective action. We even have an old adage *(To err is human)* to explain it. Human errors cannot be eliminated nor even significantly reduced simply by telling operators to be more careful. This simplistic approach does not work because we are not attacking any root cause.

The way we look at the human side of the problem has evolved during the last few decades. Industrial psychologists and human reliability professionals took command during the investigation of catastrophic accidents (Chernobyl, Challenger, and aviation accidents) and these old conceptions changed. Now, we see human errors as the symptoms of deeper causes. In other words, human errors are consequences, not causes.

Most of the time, even though accidents are classified as mechanical or other kinds of failure, the roots go back to a human who made an error. For this discussion, human error excludes deliberate actions with harmful intent; these are considered sabotage. In the FDA regulated environment, the combination human error/retraining is still indicated in the root cause and corrective action sections of many investigation reports. At this time of the twenty-first century, we can say that regulated companies are abusing human error as an explanation for faulty quality systems. This is not a book on human reliability, but any professional working with CAPA systems must become familiar with these concepts. It is essential that we stop using human error (or any of its variations) as a root cause of our quality problems. As mentioned before, we must ask why the human made the mistake.

Human errors are not a uniform collection of unwanted acts. Lack of attention plays a significant role in all categories of human error. Slips, lapses, and mistakes are all more common when situational factors (fatigue, workload, multitasking, and boredom) divert our attention. In the FDA regulated industries, these factors should be negligible; we should not be relying on memory for procedures and instructions. Batch records and device master and device history files exist for that exact purpose.

FDA and foreign regulators require the consideration of human factors during the development of medical devices. In the landmark 1996 guidance *Do It By Design—An Introduction to Human Factors in Medical Devices,* the FDA established design requirements to avoid so-called user errors. More recently the agency introduced those concepts of human reliability to drug and biotechnology manufacturers.

I highly recommend that interested professionals study some of the references included in this chapter. Although the oldest ones refer to aviation, nuclear, and industrial accidents, several recent books cover the hospital and healthcare industry, where human errors cost tens of thousands of lives every year in the United States alone.

To finish with the introduction to this critical area (by frequency and by significance), we must differentiate between error (mistakes) and defects (also known as nonconformance). Regulated companies do not recall products because there were human errors during the manufacturing process. They recall products because their quality system was unable to detect the human error and the nonconformance product was distributed, becoming an adulterated item.

Human Errors and Human Factors[5]

Human error can be defined as a departure from acceptable or desirable practices on the part of an individual resulting in unacceptable or undesirable result.

Human factors are defined as the discipline concerned with designing machines, operations, and work environments to match human capabilities, limitations, and needs. Human factors can be further defined as any factor that influences behavior at work in a way that can negatively affect the output of the process the human is involved with. This is pretty much the concept of standard work used for decades at Toyota.

When an operator does not properly execute a manufacturing step, we immediately label it human error. When we investigate the situation, inadequate training and supervision and lack of clarity in the working instruction can be factors behind the operator's mistake. As you can see, this is the same scheme we have been describing since the beginning of this chapter. Human errors and mistakes are the symptoms of causal (human) factors associated with root causes we must discover prior to solving them.

This topic of human factors falls within the field of human reliability engineering. It deals with the person–process interface and how this interaction influences the performance of people. Some authors refer to human factors as performance shaping factors (PSFs).

---

[5] Reason (1990), Dekker (2006)

Human failures can be divided into two broad categories, errors and violations:

- A human *error* is an action or decision that was not intended, that involved a deviation from an accepted standard, and that led to an undesirable outcome.

- A *violation* is a deliberate deviation from a rule or procedure.

Based on my experience, violations are rare within this industry and the vast majority of human failure can be attributed to unintended errors. Figure 3.11 depicts a classification of human errors.

The Psychology and Classification of Human Error

Errors are a predictable consequence of basic and normally useful cognitive mechanism, not random or arbitrary processes. As error expert James Reason[6] suggests, "Correct performance and systematic errors are two sides of the same coin."

Human errors are not a uniform collection of unwanted acts. Psychologists distinguish between *skill-based* slips and lapses, *rule-based* mistakes, and *knowledge-based* mistakes. *Skills* are highly practiced behaviors that we perform routinely with little conscious effort. They are literally automatic. Rule- and knowledge-based performance requires more mental involvement and conscious deliberation.

Slips and lapses occur in familiar tasks we can perform without much need for conscious attention (see Table 3.9). They are errors in the performance of skill-based behaviors, typically when our attention or memory is diverted and we fail to closely monitor the actions we are performing.

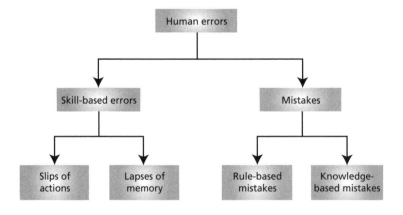

Figure 3.11 Types of human errors.

---

[6] Reason, 1990

Slips are failures in carrying out the actions of a task. They can be described as "actions-not-as-planned." Lapses cause humans to forget to carry out an action. They can be reduced by minimizing distractions and interruptions and by providing effective reminders, especially for tasks that take some time to complete or involve periods of waiting.

Mistakes are errors in rule- or knowledge-based performance. They are a more complex type of human error where we do the wrong thing believing it to be right. Mistakes include errors in perception, judgment, inference, and interpretation. Two types of mistakes exist, rule-based and knowledge-based.

Rule-based mistakes occur when our behavior is based on remembered rules or familiar procedures. We have a strong tendency to use familiar rules or solutions even when these are not the most convenient or efficient. Planning or problem solving requires that we reason from first principles or use analogies. Misdiagnosis and miscalculations can result when we use this knowledge-based reasoning.

Attention plays a significant role in all categories of human errors. Slips, lapses, and mistakes are all more common when situational factors such as fatigue, sleep loss, alcohol, drugs and illness, workload, stress, work pressure, multitasking, boredom, frustration, fear, anxiety, and anger play a role.

Violations can be defined as deliberate deviations from rules, procedures, instructions and regulations. The breaching or violating of health and safety rules or procedures is a significant cause of many accidents and injuries at work, but I don't believe that we have frequent purposeful violations of the quality system in this industry. Many companies have the documentation mechanism of planned deviations to cover such

Table 3.9 Slips and lapses of memory.

Slips (commission or execution errors)	Lapses (omission errors)
• Operating the wrong switch control or valve	• Equipment identification not recorded in the batch record
• Misordering a sequence of steps	• Omission of information that must be recorded
• Transposing digits when printing a lot number or expiration dates	• Omitting a step or series of steps from a task
• Product mixups (incorrect label, incorrect product, both incorrect)	
• Failure to detect incorrect expiration date, incorrect lot number, incorrect size, or other defect during an inspection	

circumstances. Violations are divided into three categories: routine, situational, and exceptional.

In addition to this division, there are many other ways to categorize human error. Almost every author involved in this field has developed his own list. Several of them are so complex as to require a graduate degree in human psycho-physiology to be understood. Many of us prefer simple things, so we will discuss just two of the most frequently used classifications.

Swain and Guttman (1983) divide human error into four main groups:

- Errors of *omission* (forgetting to do something)

- Errors of *commission* (doing the task incorrectly)

- *Sequence* errors (doing something out of order)

- *Timing* errors (doing the task too slow, too fast, or too late)

Reason (1990) divides between active and latent failures. *Active* failures have an immediate consequence and are usually made by front-line workers such as drivers, control room staff, or machine operators. In a situation where there is no room for error, active failures have an immediate impact on quality or health and safety.

Latent failures are made by people whose tasks are removed in time and space from operational activities (designers, decision makers, and managers). Latent failures are typically failures in management systems (design, implementation, or monitoring). Examples of human factors behind latent failures are:

- Poor design of plant and equipment

- Inadequate procedures and work instructions

- Ineffective training

- Inadequate supervision

- Inadequate staff and resources

- Ineffective communications

- Uncertainties in roles and responsibilities

In our regulated environment, most active failures trace back to some pre-condition (latent failure). We need a good tracking and trending analysis system to be able to discover what in many cases is a true cause-and-effect relationship. One of my favorite examples can clarify this point: A medical device manufacturer has a production room with two dozen identical machines producing the same kind of subassembly product. They work 24/7 and each work station is attended by only one operator who also verifies the quality of his or her job prior to sending the pieces to the storage room. The next operation suffers from frequent defective subassembly products sent from the production room and this situation is jeopardizing the productivity of the whole plant. For a couple of years now the level of defective subassembly has been between 2 percent and 3 percent, and the impact on scrap, productivity, and rework time is in the millions of dollars.

Nonconformance investigations always pointed to inadvertent human errors (they even created a form to document the human error in the area) corrected with retraining, awareness, and occasional termination. Nothing seemed to work and the rate of error remained steady. A simple analysis (data segmentation) revealed the real situation: almost 80 percent of the bad units were produced by two work stations independent of operator, shift, or day of the week. This concentration chart of defects also revealed that these two stations were the ones situated next to the two doors of the manufacturing room. They were all-glass doors opening to the main corridor of the plant. The consequence of this location was that both corner work stations received a lot of social visits from co-workers and obviously this represented an enormous source of distraction for operators attending these two machines.

As you can see, the latent factor creating those human errors was the layout of the facility. A simple substitution of the all-glass doors by metal doors effectively reduced the rate of defective products by more than two-thirds in just the first month. From this moment on, the defect rates for these two stations were not statistically different from the other 22 stations in the same room.

Reason[7] proposed what is known to as the "Swiss cheese model" of system failure. Every step in a process has the potential for failure. The system is analogous to a stack of Swiss cheese slices. Each hole is an opportunity for a process to fail, and each of the slices is a "defensive layer" in the process against potential error impacting the results. An error may allow a problem to pass through a hole in one layer, but in the next layer the holes are in different places; the problem should be caught. For a catastrophic error to occur (a plane crash or the distribution of a pharmaceutical product with incorrect label information), the holes must align for each step in the process. This allows all defenses to be defeated and results in an error. If the layers are set up with all the holes aligned, it becomes an inherently flawed system that will allow an error to become a final product defect. Each slice of cheese is an opportunity to stop an error. The more defenses we put up, the better. The fewer the holes and the smaller the holes, the more likely you are to notice errors that do occur.

It is important to note that the presence of holes in any one slice of our quality system may cause a final defect problem. Usually, this happens only when the holes in many slices momentarily line up to permit the result of the error to escape our controls. Reason establishes that those

---

[7] Reason (2000)

holes in the defenses arise for two reasons, active failures and latent pre-existing conditions, and that nearly all adverse events result from a combination of these two sets of factors.

How to Investigate Human Errors

We must investigate "human error" as we do any other nonconformance or deviation within our quality system. We have a symptom and we must discover its causal factors (human factors in this case) in order to reach the root cause. The main point to consider is that we are fingering some of our associates as responsible for the situation, and we must allow them to express their opinions. Interviewing the workers involved is the most important method used to investigate the "human errors." When interviewing the personnel involved in the event, we are not just asking questions, we are trying to discover why this person did not follow the procedure or why this person made a decision that later created the problem. Table 7.1 contains 36 questions that can be used as guidance during the investigation of human errors. The purpose of these questions is to obtain a better understanding of the human factors surrounding the issue under investigation.

You Are Interviewing, Not Interrogating

The conversation formats usually identified with a quality audit or nonconformance investigation will range from informal conversation with witnesses to a tense confrontation with the person believed responsible for the questionable action. The division between the two extremes is not a clear-cut line of separation. The more distant people are from an incident, the less concerned they are about repercussions; the closer they are to the incident, the more stressed or concerned they become in talking about the situation. The concern can be due to knowledge of the action, actual involvement in the incident, or fear of being held responsible for the actions of others.

The objective of an effective interview is to gain knowledge and information that are pertinent to the investigation. The characteristics of a typical interview include the following:

- It is a non-threatening format and the tone is non-accusatory.
- It takes a relatively short time to complete (15 minutes to one hour).
- The conversation could be conducted with or without total privacy.
- A formal written report of the conversation should follow.

Prepare Yourself Before Initiating the Interview

An experienced interviewer understands the correct questions to ask and grasps the answers that flow from the conversation. This particular skill is enhanced by advanced study and knowledge of the topic or process being discussed. If the investigator is ignorant of the process or the specific problem, the employee can take advantage of the lack of knowledge. The assimilation of sufficient background information will allow the interview team to quickly recognize inaccurate or inconsistent answers to pertinent questions. Knowledge and competence allow the investigator to enter the interview process with more confidence and self-assurance. Many times the person being interviewed will phrase answers based upon a perception of knowledge possessed by the investigator.

Opening the Interview

The meeting is expected to begin on a friendly, yet professional, tone with no defensiveness or hostility anticipated from either party. This sense of cooperation begins with the interviewer. Arrogance, aggressiveness, and an air of superiority interfere with an investigator's ability to solicit answers and assistance from the other party of the conversation. The interviewer should expect that some nervousness, even resentment, will be evident during an interview concerning an incident that may cost a lot of money and even result in a regulatory action such as a product recall.

This attitude generally subsides within a short time and both parties can then get on with the task of resolving a problem. An initial exchange with nonspecific, generic conversation allows time for both parties to adjust to the dynamics of the beginning interview. The investigator should inform the interviewee of the identity of the persons conducting the interview and the general nature of the investigation. Inflammatory words such as "fraud" or "violation" should be replaced by "review," "analyze," "examine," "unusual things," and other phrases that generate less tension.

Control the Interview Process

While it is important to begin the interview on a friendly, non-threatening basis, it is just as important to maintain firm control over the interview process. The investigator is in charge and has a mission to accomplish: to resolve the topic of the investigation. The interview should be conducted in a business place with a minimum of distractions or potential interruptions. The conversation should be limited to the subject matter at hand.

The investigator can come prepared with a list of questions that will serve as a reminder of the topics to be discussed and specific points to be covered. The list should not become a barrier that inhibits a smooth flow of dialogue. Chapter 7 includes a form that can be used during the interview to help in the process of gathering facts and data.

Allow Sufficient Time to Answer the Question

Many times the inexperienced investigator will ask a question and immediately begin to provide the answer, all before the other person has an opportunity to speak. The goal is to listen to the response, not to articulate a response. Information is gained by asking a question and listening carefully to the response.

Silence can be a strong motivator to the flow of information. Once the question is asked, wait for the answer. Silence is an obvious clue that you are waiting for a response. Allow the person being interviewed to fill the silence with information. The more the person talks, the more information you will gain from the process. Additional conversation allows you to evaluate the completeness and accuracy of the responses and detect indicators of inconsistency.

Be Alert to Nonverbal Communication

Most people have a tendency to subconsciously react when giving intentionally fabricated answers to questions. Reactions may be subtle but easily recognized by an experienced investigator. Investigators should be alert to the following nonverbal communication clues that may be an indication of deception:

- Excessive grooming or fidgeting during the interview, especially during key questions
- Avoidance of eye contact during pertinent questions
- Preoccupation or fidgeting with other items on the desk or in the room
- Excessive nervousness, heavy breathing, or fast heartbeat

The effective investigator should not place too much reliance on any one factor but should view the overall communication patterns displayed by the individual. A single gesture or motion should not be taken out of context, but rather viewed as a part of an individual's total reaction pattern. The skilled investigator must observe and analyze such points as eye movement, body gestures, and even posture in an effort to capture the full meaning of the verbal responses given to the questions.

Ending the Interview

Investigators should paraphrase or repeat key points that come from the dialogue. This ensures that the facts are understood and that nothing has been misinterpreted. Hostility should be avoided and an effort should be made to ensure that the interview ends on a positive note.

In closing, the investigator should mention the possibility of a re-contact. This might prompt an individual to "recall an important fact." An effective technique is to re-interview a critical witness in an effort to clarify a point; this gives the person a second chance to disclose significant information that is unknown to the investigator. Many witnesses are reluctant to discuss what they really know or strongly suspect. Asking "What do you *think*...?" allows the person being interviewed to respond.

Finally, it's essential to document the result of the interview as soon as possible and give a copy to the person interviewed for review.

How Regulated Companies Deal with Human Errors

An increasing number of regulated companies are establishing specific procedures to deal with this plague of human errors. Some divert the human error investigation to human resources. Others develop a checklist to search for specific human factors that could be considered precursors to the incident under investigation. The main point here is not who is in charge of the investigation but rather what tools and knowledge they have to perform a good and effective investigation. Most regulated companies still do not "get" the human factor message and focus their investigations solely on the carelessness of their associates.

Manufacturing errors are usually costly in this industry, especially when the products involved reach the customers and must be recalled. A recent case of a pill coated with the incorrect color resulted in the dismissal of the entire crew involved with the manufacture of the batch.

An FDA inspector recently discovered some backdated information. In response to the finding, the company stated that "the employees involved will be retrained and warned that a future recurrence will have zero tolerance resulting in severe action, including possible immediate termination." Several questions arise: Why did the associates backdate the information? Did management control exist to prevent or even detect this behavior? The warning letter indicates that this was a repeat observation following two previous inspections. We may conclude that many regulated companies are not dealing appropriately with human error, and some of them are not dealing with it at all.

Root Causes Related to Human Performance

In the previous section we discussed several categories of root causes directly related to the human side of manufacturing problems. Three categories (personal performance, human reliability factors, and management and supervision) encompass many of the human factors we discuss in this chapter. Other categories (training, documents, and so on) are also directly related to employee performance.

My Own Findings Within the FDA Regulated Industry

Here is a personal account based on direct observation and analysis of dozens of FDA regulated manufacturing plants. The first interesting finding is that medical device manufacturers have a lot of benchmarking to do with drug manufacturer peers. When you walk the floor of a classic drug or biotech manufacturing facility, you see that operators have in front of them the corresponding working instructions (batch record). This interesting approach combines working instructions and manufacturing records into a single quality document.

As an example, if the working instruction requires a mix between 30 and 60 minutes, the document will allow space to record when the mix started and when it was stopped (time on_____ / time off_____). This format has several advantages:

- The operator need not memorize how many minutes the mixer must be running.

- Writing down those times allows the worker and auditors to double check that the requirement was meet.

- It this step is judged to be critical, a second operator can verify its correctness.

- Further audit of the document (by manufacturing and finally by quality assurance) will provide additional opportunities to detect any error before the product is released to the market.

By contrast, when you walk the floor of most medical device manufacturers, no matter how high-tech their devices (from gloves or dental floss to highly sophisticated life-sustaining machines), you rarely see an employee reading and following a working instruction. Most of the time, the instructions are not concurrently used during manufacturing steps. An operator deprived of these critical instruments must rely on memory. When errors occur, warn the employee for not following procedure and retrain them. Nobody asks what happened at the exact moment when they had the lapse that created this defect.

Improving working instruction and records is the first crucial step you must take if you want to reduce human errors and mistakes. Very few companies (I only know one case) actually have formal training for document writers. The result is the perpetuation of ill-written procedures and working instructions filled with incorrect or incomplete information. We must recover the essence of a GMP-regulated environment. The starting point must be better manufacturing instructions. Following are just a few examples of badly written instructions:

- Mix well.

- Stick together for a few seconds.

- Verify all parameters.

The second key observation relates to the training system. It must be the second observation, because how do you effectively train someone in a procedure that is not clear? Chapter 5 includes an in-depth discussion of this topic, but here are some important thoughts:

- Today, most training provided to operators and technicians is merely the reading of less-than-perfect material (SOP, working instructions, and so on).

- Almost never is there *real* training material (such as PowerPoint presentations and flowcharts) or discussion of the material with trainees.

- Training conditions are far from ideal, taking place at the end of a work shift or conducted by less-than-adequate instructors without any pedagogical background.

- Almost nobody has a formal process to measure the effectiveness of training efforts and the only factor considered during human error investigations is the existence of a training sheet sign-off. If the employee has signed this piece of paper, training is immediately discounted as a causal factor for this event.

The third critical item is the lack of adequate supervision. Merriam-Webster's dictionary defines supervision as "the action, process, or occupation of supervising. It also defines it as a critical watching and directing (as of activities or a course of action)." In today's manufacturing environment within FDA regulated industries, it is difficult to find a supervisor who meets that definition. Supervising dozens of operators, spending hours every day in unproductive meetings, and dealing with bureaucracy (time card revision and adjustment, payroll, and so on) are just some of the reasons explaining the lack of adequate and effective supervision. We can add to this the fact that the supervisor's office is often far from his workers, which makes the supervisory function even more difficult.

Regarding these last two items, there is no difference between drug and devices manufacturers. Both have the same urgent opportunities related to training and effective supervision.

How to Reduce the Probability of Human Error
Using the CAPA concepts, those mitigation efforts have two parts:

- The preventive part must encompass important human factors such as better supervision, better procedures and working instructions, and more effective training efforts. Make your processes and your documents as error proof as you can. Do not hesitate to overuse mistake-proofing features also known by the Japanese term of *poka-yoke.*

- For the reactive part you must improve your investigations. Don't accept human error as the root cause; dig into the human factors and think twice before use retraining as a corrective action.

Let's talk about the use of retraining in the CAPA context. The definition of retrain is *to train again*. Every time I see retraining under the corrective or preventive action sections of CAPA documentation, I ask myself the same question: What is the difference between this (re)training and the original training?

If retraining is the corrective action, the original training must be the root cause of the problem we are trying to fix (remember the definition of root cause). In other words, our original training was not effective. If we retrain with the same content, the same instructor, and the same conditions, why would it be effective this time?

Companies often act as if workers make mistakes simply because they forget the instructions. They believe that retraining will help workers to not forget in the future. This lack of understanding of human error is one of the root causes of our lack of effectiveness when trying to fix human-caused defects. To succeed at error control and reduction, we must consider the influence the following factors have on behavior and performance:

- Design of plant and equipment
- Information content and format (procedures and work instructions)
- Training
- Method of work: Supervision and management controls (including adequate resources and clear roles and responsibilities)
- Communications

Do not operate from memory. Read, execute, and document is the best recipe to minimize most of the human error created by lapses of memory. Finally but not less important, we must monitor the performance of the human involved in our process. Simple statistical tools such as the analysis of proportions or chi-squared can help. The methodic identification of the best performer (who can be used for benchmarking purposes) and of the not-so-best can help the organization to improve whole processes, from job description adequacies to the best way to deliver effective training.

As stated in the previous section, there are three areas in which we must concentrate our effort to effectively and dramatically reduce the impact of the so-called human error in the bottom line of the FDA regulated industries. For doing the right thing the first time, we need:

a. Better *documents* (working instructions, specifications, and procedures) with clear, complete, and comprehensive instructions

   b. Better *training* to ensure that workers understand why they are doing what they are doing, why they always must follow instructions, and what happens when instructions are not followed

   c. Better *supervision* to ensure that workers always follow procedures and working instructions while performing any function under a GMP-regulated environment

We learned that lack of attention and lapse of memory play a significant role in all categories of human error. In FDA-regulated industries, these factors should be negligible because workers are not supposed to rely on memory for correct performance. Batch records, device master, and history files exist for a purpose. If you want to improve processes performed by humans at some level, you must remember what Reason (1990) wrote:

- Fallibility is part of the human condition
- We can't change the human condition
- We can change the conditions under which people work
- Human beings will always make errors
- Naming, blaming, and shaming have no remedial value

Table 3.10 contains recommendations for investigating human errors.

Table 3.10 Human error investigation and prevention Do's and Don'ts.

Do	Don't
• Investigate every human error to its root causes	• Use human error as a root cause
• Search for precursors of the human error (such as working from memory)	• Use retraining as the default corrective action for human failures
• Improve your working instructions and records by enhancing document format (imperative tone, graphic elements, clear and comprehensive content)	• Assume that your employees are lazy and careless about their jobs
• Improve your training system	
• Measure the effectiveness of your training efforts	

3.3 CAPA PLAN: CORRECTIVE AND PREVENTIVE ACTIONS TO FIX ROOT CAUSES

Once we arrive at the most probable causes behind our problems, it is time to develop an effective plan to prevent the recurrence of those causes. The best root cause investigation is worthless if the identified causes are not fixed. These plans must cover the following four sequential elements:

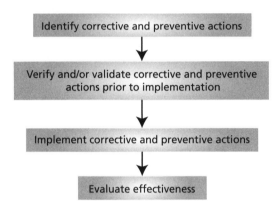

The elaboration of an adequate CAPA plan requires time. Most companies do not recognize this and that may be one of the main reasons why most CAPA systems are ineffective. One or two weeks seems to be an adequate period in which to decide the most effective way to attack the identified root causes. During this time one can evaluate where else the actions can be applied. If the corrective action is to clarify document X, the common inadequate preventive action would be to evaluate whether other documents must be clarified. The correct approach must be to perform such evaluation during the one- or two-week period described above and then write the preventive action as "clarify documents Y and Z," which were found with the same kind of problem. *Analyze, evaluate, assess,* and so on are not adequate corrective or preventive actions.

3.3.1 Establish Effective Corrective and Preventive Actions

For each root cause identified, we must generate an adequate corrective and/or preventive action. Section 1.3 has a detailed discussion of corrective versus preventive. The key point is that one must be sure that every identified root cause is covered in the CAPA plan. Many times there are several root causes and corrective actions address only one of them.

Another gray area of responsibility has to do with who should prepare the CAPA plan. It encompasses the identification of corrective and/or preventive actions, their verification and/or validation (prior to implementation), their implementation, and finally the evaluation of the plan's effectiveness. Usually the person best positioned to prepare a good CAPA plan is the one who did the investigation and discovered the root cause, but the plan must also be a team effort.

Each corrective or preventive action included in the CAPA plan must include a detailed description of every single action to be taken and an explanation on how the action will avoid the recurrence (or occurrence, if working with a preventive action) of the identified root cause. The plan must also include a description how the action will be validated or verified as well as details about its implementation (when and by whom). If the implementation is not immediate (something common in our industry), some interim actions must be included to minimize the risk of recurrence while the corrective action is implemented. Finally, for each corrective action we must always consider whether that action can be extended to other products/processes/systems not yet affected by this root cause. If the answer is affirmative, a preventive action must be created to prevent the same cause from acting elsewhere.

If you have root causes that already acted, you must have corrective actions. If you can extend the corrective actions to other places, then you will also have some preventive actions. On the other hand, if you only have potential root causes, you cannot have corrective actions; therefore, only preventive actions will be implemented.

3.3.2 Validation and Verification Prior to Implementation

Once the team decides how to fix the identified root causes, we must make sure that the proposed corrective and/or preventive actions will work, achieving the desired results from implementation. The medical device regulation includes this requirement under §820.100(a)(4) *"Verifying or validating the corrective and preventive action to ensure that such action is effective and does not adversely affect the finished device."* Comment 163 of the medical devices regulation preamble states that *"preventive, as well as corrective, action must be verified or validated"* and remarks that *"this definition makes the regulation consistent with ISO 9001:1994."*

In simple terms, we can say that there is a lot of confusion with the meaning of this section of the regulation. Remember that the medical devices regulation is considered the gold standard for CAPA. A number of companies interpret this section to require evaluation of the effectiveness of all corrective actions prior to implementation, which is impossible.

If the corrective or preventive action does affect any validated item (for example, a validated test method, a validated piece of equipment, or a validated process) then we must perform some validation work in order to secure permission to implement the action. Do not perform a validation simply because it is a corrective or preventive action; validate because your procedures and your quality system require that such action must be validated prior to implementation.

If our preventive action is to change the current visual inspection to a sophisticated electronic inspection, we must validate the inspection device to ensure that the new inspection process will consistently produce a result meeting its predetermined specifications. In this specific case, it means that the electronic eye will detect nonconformances with a predetermined confidence level.

On the other hand, if our corrective or preventive action consists of merely a clarification of some written instruction, without a major change to a process, then a validation is not necessary. The document will be changed through a formal change control process that establishes who can change the document, who must approve it, and what training requirements are associated to it. This rigorous control of the proposed change can be considered the verification of the adequacy of the change.

As part of the justification for the implementation, you must also discuss why the proposed change will not produce adverse effects on the product. If you decide to change a component, several kind of studies will be needed depending upon the product (stability, biocompatibility, and so on).

When a proposed action affects the design of medical devices, some design verification and/or validation work may be required. FDA regulation also requires that all software changes shall be validated. The FDA's analysis of 3140 medical device recalls conducted between 1992 and 1998 reveals that 242 of them (7.7 percent) were attributable to software failures. Of those software-related recalls, 192 (or 79 percent) were caused by software defects introduced when changes were made to the software after its initial production and distribution. Software validation and other related good software engineering practices discussed in this guidance are a principal means of avoiding such defects and resultant recalls.[8]

Therefore, the CAPA plan document must include:

- Description of the actions to be taken

- When it will be implemented and who is responsible for that implementation

- Effectiveness evaluation: how, when, and by whom

3.3.3 Implementation of Corrective and Preventive Actions

A frequent observation issued by FDA inspectors is that corrective and preventive actions were not implemented. To avoid this embarrassing problem, every regulated company needs a clear accountability of

---

[8] General Principles of Software Validation; Final Guidance for Industry and FDA Staff (2002).

responsibilities as well as an adequate tracking system to verify the implementation of each corrective or preventive action.

3.4 EFFECTIVENESS EVALUATION

3.4.1 Verifying That Solutions Worked

Finally, it is time to determine the effectiveness of these corrective or preventive actions. Talking in terms of problems and solutions, we must verify that the solutions worked. Two main elements here are how and when the verification is accomplished.

One of my favorite things to do at the beginning of a CAPA training session is to ask participants what and how the effectiveness of implemented actions is evaluated. Most participants mention that an action is effective if the problem does not recur. Rarely someone defines it correctly as the lack of recurrence of the root causes. Once we define what a corrective or preventive action is (the action that attacked the root cause), everyone understands that the effectiveness relates to causes, not to symptoms or problems.

If similar symptoms are observed, do not jump to the conclusion that the action was not effective. To be able to conclude this, you must first identify the root causes of this repeated symptom. If you reach the same cause, then you can conclude that the previous action was ineffective. If you discover that the problem this time was the result of a different root cause (a common situation), then your previous action is not in question. Within the same line of reasoning, sometimes you investigate a new problem and discover that the situation was created by a root cause you already fixed. In this case, you have evidence that the previous corrective or preventive action was not effective.

There are also some misunderstandings related to effectiveness verification. Some companies document that the action was implemented and not whether the action worked. If the action is not implemented, it does not have a chance to be effective; the implementation verification (discussed in the previous section) is a different concept. At this point of the CAPA cycle, the quality system asks for evidence that the implemented corrective or preventive action was effective and that the intended objective was accomplished.

Root causes are detected through the symptoms they produce. Therefore, the way to determine whether a corrective action was effective is to analyze the process that root cause acted upon. A typical question here is how long it takes to verify the effectiveness of the actions. Some companies have a fixed period of time (three months, six months, or one year); others take a more correct approach by linking that period of time to the frequency of the process being fixed.

A rule of thumb I like to use is the "double digit" rule. It requires having at least ten repetitions of the process where the corrective or preventive action was applied prior to establishing whether the action was effective. If we use a fixed period (for example three months) and the process is performed monthly, we will have only three results (in the best case) to determine such effectiveness. Statistically there is a large probability that those first three repetitions are OK simply by chance even though the action did not work. By extending the evaluation to at least ten repetitions, we maximize our confidence level. With ten good results, we can be confident that the action worked.

The documentation of the effectiveness evaluation should be generated along with the rest of the CAPA plan. Once we document the implementation of the action, the only remaining (open) task for the plan will be the effectiveness evaluation.

3.4.2 Training Effectiveness

Training is a critical component in any organization's strategy, but FDA-regulated companies rarely evaluate the impact of their training programs. *The management of effective training* provides the overall structure needed to ensure that training programs have processes in place to support FDA-regulated operations. Organizations that monitor training effectiveness and strive to improve weaknesses are consistently the best performers. It is important to develop methodologies to measure, evaluate, and continuously improve training.

Very often, the training function is seen as an expenditure center rather than as one of the most critical activities in any organization, especially in highly regulated environments such as nuclear, aerospace, medical, and pharmaceutical. In these industries training results must be measured. Incorporating selected training metrics into a reporting strategy can help demonstrate the real value of training. Measurements that consider performance improvements can provide a benchmark for training effectiveness.

A very important consideration is that most of the corrective or preventive actions are related with some training efforts, and therefore the effectiveness of these training actions must be evaluated. However, for most companies the only record generated from training activities is the attendance sheet itself. When evaluating the possible impact of training during nonconformance investigations, they merely determine whether the personnel involved in the failure signed the corresponding training roster. If so, they conclude that training can be discounted as a root cause of the situation. Training effectiveness is not an explicit requirement of FDA regulations, but the FDA has expectations regarding these topics that are included in several guidance documents. The agency's expectation is that firms must evaluate the effectiveness of their personnel training because it is a direct indicator of the robustness of the firm's quality system.

Quality data (complaints, failure investigations, audits, record reviews, and so on) must be used to assess both training needs and effectiveness. Human errors must be detected, trended, investigated, and corrected. Do not use retraining as a corrective action.

The FDA Guidance for Industry: Quality Systems Approach to Pharmaceutical CGMP Regulations [09/2006] states that "under a quality system, managers are expected to establish training programs that include the following:

- *Evaluation of training needs*
- *Provision of training to satisfy these needs*
- **Evaluation of effectiveness of training**
- *Documentation of training and/or re-training"*

Evaluation of effectiveness of training is also a requirement of ISO 13485:2003 and it is part of most of the foreign regulations pertaining to this type of industry. As if we need more reasons for the evaluation of training, here are a few others:

- To justify the existence and budget of the training department by showing how it contributes to the organization's objectives and goals
- To decide whether to continue or discontinue training programs
- To gain information on how to improve future training programs
  - Physical facilities, schedule, materials, food
  - Material contents, instructors, and so on

The Kirkpatrick Model for Training Effectiveness Evaluation[9]

More than half a century ago, Donald L. Kirkpatrick introduced a four-step approach to training evaluation. His four steps have become commonly known in the training field as Level One, Level Two, Level Three, and Level Four Evaluation. Table 3.11 reflects these four levels of evaluation.

Level One: Reaction

Kirkpatrick defines this first level of evaluation as determining "how well trainees liked a particular training program," "measuring the feelings of trainees," or "measuring the customer satisfaction." He outlines the following guidelines for evaluating reaction:

1. Determine what you want to learn.
2. Use a written comment sheet covering those items determined in step 1.
3. Design the form so that reactions can be tabulated and quantified.

---

[9] Kirkpatrick & Kirkpatrick (2006, 2007)

Table 3.11 The four levels of the Kirkpatrick model.

Levels	What	When
1. Reaction	Did they like it?	Upon completion of the training
2. Learning	Did they learn it?	Before and after training
3. Behavior	Did they use it?	Before and after training
4. Results	Did they produce measurable business results?	Before and after training

4. Obtain honest reactions by making the forms anonymous.

5. Encourage the trainees to write additional comments not covered by questions that were designed to be tabulated and quantified.

Kirkpatrick suggests also measuring the reaction of the training managers and other qualified observers. An analysis of the two groups would give the best indication of the effectiveness of the program at this first level of training evaluation.

Level Two: Learning

Kirkpatrick defines learning as "attitudes that were changed, and knowledge and skills that were learned." He outlines the following guidelines to evaluate learning:

1. The learning of each trainee should be measured so that quantitative results can be determined.

2. A before-and-after approach should be used so that any learning can be related to the program.

3. Where practical, a control group not receiving the training should be compared with the group that received the training.

4. Where practical, the evaluation results should be analyzed statistically so that learning can be proved in terms of correlation or level of confidence.

In addition to using written and oral examinations and performance tests, Kirkpatrick suggests that if a program is carefully designed, learning can be fairly and objectively evaluated while the training session is being conducted. For example, individual performance of a skill being taught and discussions following a role-playing situation can be used as evaluation techniques.

Level Three: Behavior (the Transfer of Training)

Realizing that "there may be a big difference between knowing principles and techniques and using them on the job," Kirkpatrick suggests that the following five requirements must be met for change in behavior to occur:

1. Desire to change

2. Knowledge of what to do and how to do it

3. The right job climate

4. Help in applying what was learned during training

5. Rewards for changing behavior

Kirkpatrick outlines the following guidelines for evaluating training programs in terms of behavioral changes on the job:

1. A systematic appraisal should be made of on-the-job performance on a *before-and-after* basis.

2. The appraisal of performance should be made by one or more of the following groups (the more the better):

   • The person receiving the training,

   • The person's supervisor,

   • The person's subordinates (if any),

   • The person's peers or other people thoroughly familiar with his or her performance.

3. A statistical analysis should be made to compare performance before and after and to relate changes to the training program.

4. The post-training appraisal should be made three months or more after the training so that the trainees have an opportunity to put into practice what they have learned. Subsequent appraisals may add to the validity of the study.

5. A control group (not receiving the training) should be used.

Kirkpatrick notes that *"measuring changes in behavior resulting from training programs involves a very complicated procedure."* Nevertheless, it is worthwhile if training programs are to increase in effectiveness and their benefits are to be made clear to top management. He also recognizes that few training managers have the background, skill, and time to engage in extensive evaluations, and he suggests they call on specialists, researchers, and consultants for advice and help.

Level Four: Results (The Impact of Training on the Business)

Based on the premise that "the objectives of most training programs can be stated in terms of results such as reduced turnover, reduced costs, improved efficiency, reduction in grievances, increase in quality and quantity of production, or improved morale," Kirkpatrick concludes "it would be best to evaluate training programs directly in terms of results desired."

He recognizes there are so many complicating factors that it is extremely difficult, if not impossible, to evaluate certain kinds of programs in terms of results. He recommends that training managers evaluate in terms of reaction, learning, and behavior first and then consider tangible business results. He also cautions that due to the difficulty in the separation of variables—that is, how much of the improvement is due to training as compared to other factors—it is very difficult to measure results that can be attributed directly to a specific training program.

From Kirkpatrick's experience with level four evaluations, he concludes that it is probably better to use the personal interview rather than a questionnaire to measure results. Also, measures on a before-and-after basis can provide evidence (but not necessarily proof) that the business results are directly attributed to the training even though other factors might have been influential.

Chapter 6 includes an example of training evaluation applied to an internal CAPA program certification.

3.5 MANAGEMENT OF THE CAPA SYSTEM

Management of the CAPA system is perhaps the most compelling task pharmaceutical, medical devices, and biological companies face today. The requirement is simple: implementing an efficient CAPA system as part of an overall quality management system. Lack of compliance with the different CAPA system elements is the top observation from worldwide regulatory inspections. Weakness of the CAPA system is a true indicator of the overall regulatory and quality health of the organization. Daniel and Kimmelman (2008)[10] cited three causes for this weakness:

- Overloading of the CAPA processes
- Inadequate resources applied to the processes
- Inadequate follow-up of corrective actions

I agree with these reasons and may add a fourth: the over-customization of CAPA processes. It is almost impossible to understand the CAPA system and processes of any regulated company only by reading its CAPA documents. For some unknown reason, each regulated firm tries

---

[10] Daniel and Kimmelman (2008)

to complicate CAPA as much as possible. The unfortunate result is constant violation of its own procedures. Chapter 5 contains a discussion of the top ten symptoms of inadequate CAPA systems and some recommendations for fixing them.

To complete the introduction to this section, I will share with you the two indispensable items needed to build an effective CAPA system: *time* and *resources*. Good CAPA processes require both of them and management is ultimately responsible for efficient quality processes, including CAPA processes.

3.5.1 CAPA System Structure

Most companies do not have a formal structure devoted to CAPA processes and almost anyone can perform CAPA investigations. In most companies, someone from within the quality department acts as a reviewer of the investigation, leading to the back and forth of investigation reports. Reporting to management is usually in the form of useless metrics regarding how many reports are past due.

Best practices for the CAPA systems include the following:

- Dedication of full-time investigators, most often organized in cross-functional teams
- Creation of multi-departmental boards to evaluate investigations, CAPA plans, and effectiveness checks
- Creation of a CAPA management function in charge of documenting and monitoring CAPA metrics and activities

All of these are key improvement factors along with establishing risk management tools to develop and maintain an efficient CAPA system.

3.5.2 CAPA Process Metrics

Trending is an important tool for reporting and controlling quality processes. It is also a main requirement of the quality management system. If you do not measure your processes, you cannot manage or improve them. The only metrics most regulated firms use are those related to timeliness, and most of them are useless metrics because time requirements are rarely risk based. A company will establish, for example, a 30-day period to complete investigations, regardless of any priority criterion. This is one of the ten diseases affecting our CAPA systems; more on this topic can be found in Chapter 5.

Regulators' expectation is that CAPA processes be completed in a reasonable timeframe, commensurate with the risk and the magnitude of the event. Normally four timeframes can be established and monitored:

a. Detection of the problem and initiation of the nonconformance investigation

b. Completion of the root cause investigation, including documentation and approval of the report

c. Preparation of the CAPA plan

d. Evaluation of the effectiveness of the implemented corrective or preventive actions

Firms must define adverse trends for each quality metric. When an adverse trend is identified, an investigation should be initiated to identify the root causes. From the point of view of continuous improvement and the health of the quality system, the most important information is obtained from the analysis of root causes and the evaluation of the effectiveness of corrective and preventive actions. In the first case, a simple Pareto chart can help to monitor the prevalent root causes.

Other useful metrics can be:

• Number of investigations opened during this month

• Number of investigations overdue during this month

• Number of investigations closed during this month

• Cycle time of investigations closed during this month

3.5.3 Risk Management and the CAPA System

Most of the discussion of this topic was included at the beginning of Chapter 3. Following are a few critical points we must remember:

• Always link your CAPA process to the risk (importance and magnitude) of the event.

• Provide enough resources to investigate, review, and manage your CAPA system.

• Provide enough time to complete CAPA activities.

• Professionalize your CAPA functions (use full-time investigators).

• Establish multi-functional boards for investigation reports evaluation and for CAPA plan activities.

• Always consider CAPA one of your most critical processes.

3.5.4 Management of External CAPA

When the nonconformance relates to suppliers, there are differences in respect to the internal CAPA system. Perhaps the main difference is that the timeframe for completing the investigation and implementing corrective or preventive action is out of our control. Most suppliers to the FDA regulated industry have a poor quality system and very low understanding of the CAPA system.

In most cases, regulated companies will document the detected nonconforming situation including corrections and then request a full investigation and CAPA from the vendor. Contact with the vendor is established through a supplier quality group, which is responsible for getting acceptable CAPA documentation from the vendor in order to close the CAPA event. It is not recommended to apply to those vendor investigations the same timeframe used for the internal investigation reports (for example, 20 or 30 days) because you will have no control over it.

Best practices for external CAPA include:

- "Educate" your supplier base about the CAPA system criticality and the need for timely responses to nonconformance investigations and CAPA issues.

- Include explicit CAPA responsibilities and responsiveness within the contract or quality agreement your company must establish with each of your suppliers.

- Tie the timeline for supplier response to risk and the magnitude of the nonconformance.

- Establish responsiveness metrics to measure and evaluate each supplier.

- Be ready to help suppliers with resources if your external CAPA becomes stagnant.

- Give top priority to the supplier CAPA system during audits.

4

Documenting CAPA

4.1 CONTENT OF THE INVESTIGATION REPORT/CAPA PLAN REPORT

The investigation report and CAPA plan should include the following elements:

EVENT INFORMATION

Affected product / process / system:

Date occurred:

Date discovered:

Date reported:

DESCRIPTION OF THE ISSUE

What happened?

What should have happened? (What is the specification, or instruction?)

Where did it happen?

How was the event discovered?

When was it discovered?

Who discovered it?

IMMEDIATE ACTIONS TAKEN

What was done after the event was discovered?

INITIAL IMPACT ASSESSMENT

Does this situation impact other products, equipment, raw materials, components, and / or systems?

If there is product involved in this event, identify and evaluate lots or batches run before and/or after the event under investigation.

Has any affected material already been released/distributed to customers?

Risk classification of the event:

INVESTIGATION DETAILS

a. Problem definition

- Background and historical data (trend analysis)
- Chronology of the event
- Comparison matrix (Is–Is Not)

b. Current barrier analysis

c. Root cause analysis

- Causal factors
- Potential root causes
  - Cause-and-effect diagram
  - Fault tree analysis

CONCLUSION ABOUT ROOT CAUSES

What are the most probable root causes of this event?

Root cause classification of the event:

CAPA PLAN

a. **Correction/Containment Action.**

b. **Corrective Action.** Must have at least one identified CA for each root cause already identified. Each corrective action must include the following information:

- How this action will avoid the recurrence of the identified root causes.
- Recommended interim action, if the proposed CA is not immediate.
- Implementation verification: how, when, and by whom.
- Effectiveness check: how, when, and by whom.
- Can this action be extended to other products/processes/systems not yet affected by this root cause? If yes, open a preventive action.

c. **Preventive Action.** Should have at least one identified PA for each potential root cause already identified. Each preventive action must include the following information:

- How this action will avoid the occurrence of the identified potential root causes.
- Recommended interim action, if the proposed PA is not immediate.
- Implementation verification: how, when, and by whom.
- Effectiveness check: how, when, and by whom.

FINAL DISPOSITION—APPROVAL OF INVESTIGATION

a. What is the final decision taken regarding the affected product/process/system?

b. Approval signatures.

EXECUTIVE SUMMARY/ABSTRACT

Provide a short summary of the investigation facts and results, including a description of the event and the list of correction, corrective and/or preventive actions taken.

4.2 COMPLIANCE WRITING

In Table 4.1 are some basic recommendations to be followed when writing a compliance report. The list of Don'ts to be avoided when writing investigation reports or some other type of CAPA documents is long. The first recommendation is to avoid passion. Investigation reports in particular and regulatory documents in general must state facts and data only. Speculations, perceptions, and opinions do not have a place in the compliance writing world.

Following are some examples taken from real investigation reports. Certainly there are more than facts and data in these phrases:

"This product is *always* running on the low side of the specifications"

"…this was an *extremely* low failure…"

"Two *consecutive* lots gave OOS very high"

"…Due to *noncompliance* with batch record instructions"

"This product is *always* running *very close* to the lower specification limit"

"Assessment time exceeded: Situation was reported but assessment was not completed on the two-day period required *due to multiple priorities in the area*"

"After a *while*, the recorder…"

"This was a *real* isolated incident…"

Table 4.1 Compliance writing Do's and Don'ts.

Do	Don't
Clarity • Use concrete and specific words • Use active verbs • Use standard English words • Be positive **Readability** • Replace long words with short words • Break long sentences **Economy** • Cut empty verbs • Cut unnecessary prepositions • Cut redundancy **Correctness** • Check word choice • Check grammar • Check punctuation • Proofread	• Use inflammatory statements • Be judgmental • Assign blame • Speculate about liabilities or lack of compliance • Make a broad conclusion • Offer unsupported opinions, perceptions, and speculations • Make personal references • Use loaded words • Sensationalize (this was a *critical* failure) • Use unnecessary details • Guess • Exaggerate • Be imprecise • Use absolutes such as always, never, or totally • Use alarm words such as bad, catastrophic, critical failure, or negligent

5

The Ten Biggest Opportunities of the CAPA System and How to Fix Them

This chapter describes a decalogue containing the ten most common opportunities of the CAPA system and how to fix them. Real examples from each opportunity are analyzed and best practices for each one are discussed.

5.1 TIMELINESS (LACK OF)

There is a tremendous variability regarding timeframes the regulated companies establish to deal with several aspects of the CAPA system. These may range from no time limits (a rare occurrence) to 30-day limits (calendar or business), including the effectiveness check of corrective actions. The FDA has no requirement for time limits, mentioning only the term *reasonable* in a note published in 1997 as part of the Human Drug CGMP Notes by the Division of Manufacturing and Product Quality, Office of Compliance of the CDER.

> "The CGMP regulations, at 21 CFR §211.192, establish the requirement for an investigation, but do not explicitly state a time interval for completing it, including the preparation of a report. Our expectation for "closure" of a failure investigation (including any other "unexplained discrepancy") is that the investigation be conducted and reported in a reasonable time. The *Barr* decision called this "timely" (see paragraph 23 of that decision).
>
> We see both the 30-day time period in the court decision and the 20-day time period in the referenced inspectional guide as being reasonable or timely; both are guidance and not requirements. The times differ because the Court addressed an investigation by a manufacturing site having a laboratory, whereas the guide addresses investigation in the laboratory only. We see the investigation in the manufacturing site that has a laboratory including other manufacturing aspects along with laboratory aspects.

In discussing this topic, it may be helpful to point out what would not be reasonable, like performing an investigation but not progressing to a decision point as recorded in a final report/ decision document, delaying a decision on investigation findings beyond the expiration date of the lot(s) in question, or delaying/ excluding the investigation from GMP or application related records which require their inclusion."

When an investigation is reaching its self-imposed time limit, management often increases pressure on investigators and reviewers. The result is that most investigations are inadequately completed but closed without exceeding the time limit. I enjoy asking during training sessions which is more important for management: closing on time or closing once the investigation is adequately completed. The honest response is always the same: on time. Returning to the time limit, we should differentiate among the three main stages of the CAPA system.

Investigation

Typically, the investigation stage begins with the detection of an issue and extends until the most probable root cause has been found. This stage is important because until we know the causes of the problem, everything is under suspicion. After an out of specification is obtained during the test of an in-process material, components used for manufacture, personnel involved in the manufacture and analysis, and instruments and equipment used for manufacture are potential root causes that can be discarded only after the investigation has been performed. One of the first steps of any investigation is to establish whether the situation we are dealing with could be impacting other products or, even worse, our customers and patients. A typical example is when we discover an instrument out of calibration. In this situation, an assessment should be performed considering the worst case scenario: The equipment could have been out of tolerance since the last successful calibration, and all production material related to this equipment since then must be evaluated. This initial evaluation of the situation, based on the preliminary data and evidence available at this point, should be the first task when initiating any investigation. Details of the content of this initial impact assessment are discussed in sections 3.1.2 and 3.1.3.

Investigation Best Practices

- Performing a risk assessment of the issue considering several risk factors (refer to Chapter 3.1.2). High-risk investigations will have priority over low-risk situations.

- Including a timeframe for completing the investigation (from the date when the issue was discovered to the approval of the investigation). A reasonable timeframe for this phase would be 20 calendar days for high-risk situations and 30 calendar days for medium-risk situations. Good investigations need time. Most corrections are implemented during this period, some of them even before the formal opening of the investigation.

CAPA Plan

Once the root causes are known, it is time to decide how we can avoid their recurrence. The best investigation can become a waste of effort if no adequate corrective actions are established and implemented. Unfortunately, most firms only develop and implement spot fixes. The CAPA plan must consider the three main elements extensively covered in several other sections of this book:

a. Corrective action

b. Interim corrective action

c. Preventive action

CAPA Plan Best Practices

- Definitively, time is needed to analyze and develop effective corrective actions. Between two and four weeks is a reasonable timeframe to develop the CAPA plan.

- Avoid the use of "analyze," "evaluate," "assess," or any synonyms as preventive actions. Most of the time, such analysis and evaluation do not reach any further. It is one of the main reasons for the lack of real preventive action in our industry. These assessments (for example "evaluate whether any other document must be changed") are performed during this CAPA plan timeframe and their results (that is, "seven documents must be changed") is the true preventive action to be implemented.

Effectiveness Evaluation

The timeframe for this evaluation must be established case by case. Some firms establish a fixed period of time (one month, three months, and so on) for all effectiveness evaluations instead of correlating the period of time with the frequency of the process under evaluation. I have learned about a few companies that require completion of the entire CAPA process within 30 days. This includes the investigation of the event to discover the root cause, the generation and implementation of corrective and preventive actions, and the evaluation of their effectiveness. Without question, these cases represent the poorest CAPA systems I have seen, and the main factor is management's lack of understanding of the CAPA system.

Effectiveness Evaluation Best Practices

Use the "double-digits" rule of thumb: Allow enough time to permit the evaluation of at least ten repetitions of the process under evaluation. If the process runs approximately every month, then one year could be a reasonable period of time to determine whether the corrective action was effective in preventing the recurrence of the cause. If the process is performed weekly, then three months should be enough. For a daily process, one month is a good period of time to establish the effectiveness of a corrective action.

5.2 EVERYTHING IS AN ISOLATED EVENT (LACK OF ADEQUATE TRENDING)

One of the first questions to be answered at the beginning of any investigation is fundamental: Is this the first time this situation happened? At this point of time, we only know symptoms: a lot failed a QC test or a customer complained about something. The answer to the question establishes the frequency or recurrence of the situation; it is one of the main elements of risk management within the CAPA process. If this is a recurrent issue, we already have a breakdown of our CAPA system because previous incidents were either not investigated or were not properly corrected.

Examples

Most companies do not have adequate procedures for trending and very often consider events to be isolated. Recent warning letters illustrate this situation:

> "Failure to adequately establish and maintain procedures analyzing processes, work operations, concessions, quality audits reports, quality records, service records, complaints, returned product, and other sources of quality data to identify existing and potential causes of nonconforming product, or other quality problems, as required by 21 CFR §820.100(a)(1). For example, neither the Corrective and Preventive Action procedures, and Investigation Procedure nor the complaint handling procedure define the terms "trending" and "statistical methods." Defining trending and statistical methods assists in applying a consistent methodology in analyzing quality problems and adverse events. Trending and statistical methods that are not sufficiently robust may not be sensitive enough to detect significant increases in quality problems and adverse events. Furthermore, the complaint procedure indicates that quarterly trending of complaints will occur and links the trending to the CAPA procedure. However,

neither procedure establishes when quarterly complaint analysis results are considered significant enough to warrant inclusion in the company CAPA subsystem."

Other examples:

"In investigating this complaint, you considered it to be an isolated event and did not extend your investigation to product that had been distributed, even though you determined that the equipment X had been used on 93 lots from November 20, 200x through January 23, 200x, during the time when the operator involved in the complaint had been assigned to the sealing department. As this example illustrates, your firm has an established practice of considering only the number of complaints received, rather than the criticality of each complaint received, when determining whether there is a need to take preventative and/or corrective actions."

"The CGMP deviations noted during the establishment inspection, where the firm's employees failed to follow Standard Operating Procedures, do not appear to be isolated events." ... "The commonality regarding the above referenced reworks is that the firm's requests stated that personnel training and experience were factors in the product quality as well as failure to follow Standard Operating Procedures."

"Investigations of two positive sterility tests did not determine conclusive or probable root causes for the contamination. Although root causes were not determined, both investigations conclude that "the impact of the sterility test positive was isolated to the affected batch" and all other batches placed on hold when the test failures were found were released for distribution."

Requirements for trending are scattered across the different regulations and were discussed in Chapter 3, focusing on the in-conformance analysis that constitutes the basis for preventive actions.

Best Practices

- Perform a search looking for indications of a previous event. This search must cover an adequate timeframe and must be commensurate with the frequency of the process rather than a fixed period of time (for example, three or six months). In any case, be sure to evaluate at least the last ten times this process ran. Using this "double-digit" rule of thumb, if the frequency of the process is approximately every month, then one year should be a reasonable search period. If the process runs approximately every week, one quarter will be adequate.

- Always include the search query elements as part of the investigation. It's highly recommended that, as part of the review/approval process, someone should repeat the search query to verify its results. Few things are more dangerous to our credibility than an auditor finding that the "isolated" event was not so isolated.

5.3 ROOT CAUSE NOT IDENTIFIED

A common problem observed in many companies is that most nonconformance investigations point to human error or procedures not followed as the root cause of the nonconformity. As previously discussed, these are merely symptoms of deeper causes. To establish and maintain an effective CAPA system, companies must move beyond symptoms and causal factors and reach the root cause level of the problem.

This situation originated from the lack of an adequate root cause analysis process. Even though most regulated companies include many root cause tools within their investigation procedures, almost none of them require the use of the tools. It is like a wish list (tools you *could* use…). We need a root cause analysis system and management must enforce its use, not just suggest it. Training on root cause tools is not the usual main factor of a poor investigation. The main factor is the lack of application of the tools.

Examples

Following are typical examples of "root causes" that are merely symptoms:

- Human error
- Procedures not followed
- Equipment malfunction
- Improper performance
- Method not validated
- Multiple batches in process at the same time
- Clean-room gowns not used
- Equipment with expired calibration
- Out of trend point

Best Practices

- To correct this situation, the CAPA management team must avoid the use of any of the above mentioned symptoms as root cause.
- In the above examples, ask *why* the point is out of trend or *why* the method was not validated.

- One of the best tools you can use is to ask why several times until you reach a fixable root cause.

Include the requirement to use problem-solving tools as part of your investigation procedure. I recommend including the following tools:

- Chronology
- Comparison matrix
- Cause-and-effect diagram
- Fault tree analysis

5.4 CORRECTING THE SYMPTOMS INSTEAD OF THE CAUSE

Along with the abuse of human error and retraining (see Chapter 5.10), correcting the symptoms instead of the cause is perhaps the most prevalent CAPA improvement problem experienced by regulated companies. Multiple causes can create this weakness of the CAPA system. I believe that most companies simply don't understand the differences between a correction (specific spot fix) and a corrective or preventive action (attack on the root cause). From operators to middle and top level managers, they have a problem understanding key CAPA terms.

Examples

The following are simple corrections that are often disguised as corrective actions:

- Train a non-trained operator
- Reject and destroy a failing product
- Rework some nonconforming material
- Repair a piece of broken equipment
- Properly connect the alarm to the machine
- "Use as is" nonconforming products

Best Practices

- Ensure that your organization understands the meaning of and differences among correction, corrective action, and preventive action. Also be sure that workers can distinguish between symptoms and real root causes.
- Ensure that there is at least a real and adequate corrective or preventive action for each identified root cause. Formulating a simple question can help you to differentiate between correction and corrective actions: Will this corrective action avoid (prevent) the cause occurring again? If the answer is no, then you have simply a correction.

5.5 LACK OF INTERIM CORRECTIVE ACTIONS

The need for interim corrective action is one of the most unknown and unused concepts in the industry regulated by the FDA. If the corrective action cannot be implemented immediately, then we must establish interim actions to avoid the recurrence of the situation while the permanent corrective action is implemented.

Reasons for delay in the implementation of the permanent action can be several and well justified, including the need to buy and validate a piece of equipment or the need to change a written procedure. Inexcusable is the absence of some kind of interim action to cover the implementation period. Having no interim action in this situation is not acceptable. A worst-case scenario relates to those companies routinely allowing a very long period to elapse before implementing corrective action. I have learned about a few of this kind, allowing nine months or even one full year to implement the corrective or preventive action. None of them used the interim action concept.

Examples

Several customer claims were received due to missing components on a medical device kit. The current inspection is performed visually by packaging operators. The identified root cause was operator error and the corrective action was to switch to an electronic system inspection. The company allowed nine months for implementation of the new system. What interim control measures were established during those nine months? None. How many claims were received during that period? Dozens.

Interim actions this company could have taken include increasing sampling quantity or frequency and increasing inspection levels.

Best Practices

Before you approve any corrective action, always ask whether the process involving the nonconformance will be run again prior to the implementation of the corrective action. If the answer is yes, then you must request some interim action. Although interim actions must be specific to identified root causes, additional sampling or inspection and additional testing are among the most used.

5.6 ROOT CAUSES IDENTIFIED
BUT NOT CORRECTED

Try always to fix *all* the already identified root causes. Leaving "unattended" root causes today will create problems tomorrow. When you compare the root cause and the CAPA plan sections of any investigation report, very often they do not match. It is necessary to have at least one corrective action matched to every identified root cause.

Examples

The investigation report documented three root causes: lack of training, unclear document instructions, and inadequate supervision. Training and instructions were covered by corrective actions, but there was nothing related to the inadequate supervision.

Best Practices

- Do not follow the Pareto principle by fixing only the prominent cause.

- Try to fix identified causes unless you can demonstrate a lack of risk.

5.7 LACK OF TRUE PREVENTIVE ACTIONS

Most CAPA systems are really only CA systems because they do not include a preventive component. These companies are in the firefighting (corrective) mode and they lack the proactive approach that comes from the analysis of their *in-conformance* process results. Unfortunately, we must conclude that many regulated companies do not have a true CAPA system. The relationship between CA and PA establishes the maturity of the CAPA system.

Again, there is a lack of understanding of the differences between corrective action and preventive action. If the root cause is tied to a nonconformity, by definition the action to be taken must be corrective.

Examples

To evaluate whether there are other incorrect procedures. This is a typical example of preventive action observed in our industry. The correct way to operate is to make this evaluation as part of the CAPA plan and identify how many procedures are not correct. Then, the true preventive action is to change those incorrect procedures.

Best Practices

- Track and trend most significant processes based on risk.

- Monitor in-conformance results to identify developing adverse trends.

- Remember that preventive action deals with potential root causes.

- Consider other sources of preventive action such as management reviews, design reviews, and risk management reviews.

- Determine whether each corrective action can be implemented elsewhere as a preventive action (other systems, other products, and/or other processes).

- Do not use *evaluate, assess,* and *investigate* as preventive action.

5.8 LACK OF EFFECTIVENESS VERIFICATION OF THE ACTION TAKEN

A corrective action will be considered effective if it is able to avoid the recurrence of the cause. You cannot tie the evaluation of the effectiveness to the presence or absence of the symptom, because:

- The same symptom can be produced by different root causes

- The same root cause can create different symptoms

There are also misunderstandings related to the verification of effectiveness. Some companies document that the action was implemented rather than provide evidence that the action worked as intended. The evaluation of training effectiveness was discussed in Chapter 3.4.

Examples of Inadequate Verification of Effectiveness

- The corrective action was implemented

- The problem did not appear during the past three months

Best Practices

- Clearly define the evaluation of the effectiveness of the corrective and/or preventive actions.

- Establish statistically sound verification plans, or at least use the "double-digits" rule of thumb: Allow enough time to permit the evaluation of at least ten repetitions of the process under evaluation.

  – If the process runs approximately every month, then one year should be a reasonable period of time to determine whether the corrective action was effective.

  – If the process is performed approximately every week, then three months should be enough.

  – For a daily process, one month is a good period of time to establish effectiveness.

5.9 MULTIPLE CAPA SYSTEMS WITHOUT CORRELATION

Companies must identify and document relevant data sources or feeders of the CAPA system. The sources are both internal and external to the company, and the company must integrate those data sources and data elements in order to identify rising issues or developing adverse patterns.

Often this analysis is segmented by geography (domestic versus international) or other factors. The disastrous result is that no one in the organization can see the whole CAPA system picture.

Examples of Inspection Findings

- Firm's management of corrective and preventive actions (CAPA) is inadequate. Specifically, the firm is taking CAPAs under various quality data headings (incidences, nonconformities) without correlation into the firm's CAPA system, preventing accurate analysis and timely review.

- Two databases are used to handle complaints (domestic, rest of the world), with the result that management is only made aware of some complaints received.

- Corrective and preventive actions generated from internal audit observations are not included in the general CAPA database; therefore, they are not evaluated during management review meetings.

Best Practices

- Have only one CAPA system.
- Establish a meaningful metric and tracking process for your CAPA system.
- Do not forget to analyze your CAPA system by root cause categories.
- Compare and evaluate key CAPA metrics with your sister facilities.

5.10 ABUSE OF HUMAN ERROR AND RETRAINING

Even though this topic was discussed in Chapter 3.2.6, I want to include some remarks here:

- Between 80 percent and 90 percent of corrective and preventive actions taken in the FDA regulated industries are related to humans working with their processes.

- Human error is not a root cause; it is simply a symptom of a more profound cause.

- Humans are involved in all processes and fallibility is part of the human condition. Humans will always make errors.

- We can't change the human condition, but we can change the conditions under which people work.

Examples

Here are some examples of working instructions not followed by operators. In all related nonconformance investigations, the root cause was assigned to "operator error." You will notice that with these instructions, anybody will fail:

- Verify all parameters

- Mix well

- Mix slowly

- As soon as possible

- Mix for a minimum of 30 minutes

- Stick together for a few seconds

Best Practices

- There is only one: Do not allow the use of human error as a root cause. Always ask *why* the human made the mistake.

6

Developing an Internal CAPA Expert Certification

To enhance your CAPA system, I recommend that you certify your investigators and reviewers. Following is a CAPA expert certification model I developed some time ago.

6.1 CONTENT OF THE CERTIFICATION

The CAPA system certification (see Table 6.1) is a comprehensive certification course consisting of seven modules with a total duration of six days equivalent to 48 contact-hours. Approximately 30 percent of this time is be devoted to practice exercises. This certification covers the following five areas:

- Problem detection
- Problem description
- Root cause analysis
- CAPA plan
- Effectiveness evaluation

Upon completion of this certification program, participants will be able to:

- Apply a proven investigational methodology to determine the root causes of process deviations, OOS, nonconformities, and customer claims
- Implement effective corrective and preventive actions
- Write effective investigation reports
- Apply risk management tools and concepts to the CAPA system
- Establish appropriate CAPA system metrics

Table 6.1 Content of the CAPA expert certification.

Elements of the CAPA System Certification (Training Modules)	Duration (hours)
1. Regulatory Importance of CAPA	4
2. Root Cause Analysis	12
3. Effective CAPA	8
4. Human Factors	8
5. Compliance Writing	8
6. Risk Management of CAPA	4
7. CAPA Metrics and Process Trending	4
Total	48

The detailed content of each module is described below.

Module 1: Regulatory Importance of CAPA (4 h)

1. CAPA and Medical Devices Regulations
    - Key Definitions
    - U.S. FDA Regulations
    - Non-U.S. Regulations: Canada, Japan, European Community, and so on
2. The QSIT: CAPA Subsystem
3. Updated Regulatory Trends

Module 2: Root Cause Analysis (12 h)

1. Causal Factors and Root Causes
    - Root Causes Classification
2. Problem Description
    - Chronology of Events
    - Comparative Analysis: Is–Is Not matrix
    - Flowchart: Task Analysis
    - Change Analysis
3. Barrier Analysis
    - Physical Controls
    - Administrative Controls
4. Root Cause Analysis
    - Cause-and-Effect Analysis
    - FTA (Fault Tree Analysis)
    - Determining the Most Probable Root Causes

Module 3: Effective CAPA (8 h)

1. The CAPA Plan
   - Correction
   - Corrective Actions
   - Preventive Actions
2. Verification and Validation of Corrective and Preventive Actions
3. Implementation of Corrective and Preventive Actions
4. Effectiveness Evaluation
5. Dissemination of CAPA Information
6. Management of the CAPA System
7. The Ten Biggest Opportunities
   - Timeliness
   - Everything is an Isolated Event
   - Root Cause not Identified
   - Correcting the Symptoms Instead of the Cause
   - Lack of Interim Corrective Actions
   - Root Causes Identified but not Corrected
   - Lack of True Preventive Actions
   - Lack of Effectiveness Verification of the Action Taken
   - Multiple CAPA Systems without Correlation
   - Abuse of Human Error and Retraining

Module 4: Human Factors and Human Errors (8 h)

1. Human Errors and Human Factors Overview
   - Human Errors in the Industry
   - Human Errors for the FDA
   - Human Error Probabilities
   - Types of Human Errors
   - Frequency, Risk, and Trending of Human Errors
2. Investigating Human Errors
   - Casual Factors versus Root Causes
   - Barriers and Current Controls for Human Errors
   - The Memory Factor
   - Collecting Data: Interviewing and Documenting Human Errors
   - Trend and Statistical Analysis of Human Errors
   - Training Issues Related to Human Errors
   - Root Cause Analysis for Human Errors: Fault Tree Analysis
   - List of Root Causes Tied to Human Errors

3. Corrective and Preventive Actions for Human Errors
    • Determining the Best Corrective and Preventive Actions for the Identified Root Causes: How to improve procedures and working instructions
    • Verifying and/or Validating Actions
    • Implementing Actions
    • Effectiveness Evaluations for Implemented Actions

Module 5: Compliance Writing (8 h)

1. Measures of Excellence
2. Regulatory Aspects of Writing
3. Documentation Style Manual
    • Abbreviations
    • Numbers and Numerals
    • Symbols
    • Punctuation
    • Capitalization
    • Bold and Italics usage
    • Lists
    • Grammar and Usage
    • Correct and Preferred Usage of Words
4. Writing Effective Regulatory Documents
    • Sentence Construction
    • Emphasizing Text
    • Content Development
    • Organizing Information
    • Writing for Clarity
    • Writing for Economy
    • Writing for Readability
    • Writing for Correctness
5. Elements of Investigation Report

Module 6: Risk Management of CAPA (4 h)

1. Risk Management and the FDA
2. Definitions (ISO 14971: 2007 and ICH Q9)
3. What is the Quality Risk Management Process?

4. The Risk-Based Approach

5. The Quality Risk Management Process

6. The Risk Management Plans (RMP)—Integration into CAPA

7. Investigation Prioritization using Risk Management

Module 7: CAPA Metrics and Process Trending (4 h)

1. CAPA System Scorecard
   - Main CAPA Metrics
     - Nonconformance metrics
     - In-conformance metrics

2. Process Monitoring for Problem Detection
   - FDA Regulations and Definitions
   - Environmental Monitoring Process
     - Alert and Action Levels
   - Product Specification and Process Limits
   - Run Charts: Runs and Other Rules
   - Control Charts
   - Additional Tools:
     - Pre-Control Charts
     - Regression Analysis

6.2 EVALUATING THE EFFECTIVENESS OF INTERNAL CAPA TRAINING EFFORTS

The objective of this evaluation is to be able to demonstrate (with objective evidence) that the training efforts are effective. A comprehensive training effectiveness evaluation system is conducted using the four levels of the Kirkpatrick model. Each participant must complete at least three investigation reports successfully to become certified. The elements of the certification are given in Table 6.2.

The evaluation (Level 3) of each investigation report is accomplished using the CAPA assessment form included in Chapter 7.3.

Table 6.2 CAPA expert certification evaluation levels.

Elements of Certification
a. Prerequisites: minimal experience requirement and internal training
b. Evaluation of training effectiveness
1. **Reaction** (survey after each module)
2. **Learning** (exam: pre- and post-training)
3. **Behavior** (by instructor, evaluating at least three investigations per candidate to certification)
4. **Results** (measured by sponsor and certification instructor, based on pre-established metrics)
c. **Recertification** process: good CAPA practices annual refresher

6.3 CAPA CERTIFICATION EXAM EXAMPLE

Example of exam (level 2)

1. FDA expectations are that training effectiveness be assessed because
   a. It is a requirement of GMP
   b. It is a requirement for biotech products and should be evaluated for devices and drugs too.
   c. Training is a fundamental element of GMPs.
   d. All of the above.

2. Human factors are integral part of design for
   a. Biotech products
   b. Drug products
   c. Medical devices
   d. All of the above

3. The action taken to eliminate a detected nonconformity is a
   a. Preventive action
   b. Corrective action
   c. Correction
   d. All of the above

4. A rework is considered
   a. Preventive action
   b. Corrective action
   c. Correction
   d. None of the above

5. Translating a working instruction to Spanish after a recommendation is received during an external audit is a
   a. Preventive action
   b. Corrective action
   c. Correction
   d. All of the above

6. Repairing broken equipment is an example of
   a. Preventive action
   b. Corrective action
   c. Correction
   d. None of the above

7. Rewriting an erroneous document after it has caused a nonconformance is an example of
   a. Preventive action
   b. Corrective action
   c. Correction
   d. None of the above

8. Evaluating the possibility to change a procedure is a
   a. Preventive action
   b. Corrective action
   c. Correction
   d. None of the above

9. Modifying the preventive maintenance schedule of a piece of equipment after a breakdown can be considered a
   a. Preventive action
   b. Corrective action
   c. Correction
   d. None of the above

10. Changing the electric sensor of an inspection machine after an electric power outage damaged it can be considered a
    a. Preventive action
    b. Corrective action
    c. Correction
    d. None of the above

11. Describe the basic elements of an investigation report.

12. Regulations and guidances: Are they the same? Explain your answer.

13. Define and describe the elements of the CAPA system.

14. Why we can say that the CAPA system is a closed-loop system?

15. How can we verify whether training was effective?

7

CAPA Forms

The following four forms are provided in this chapter:

1. *Event Description and Investigation.* It includes all details that must be included as part of the investigation, from the description of the event to the conclusion of the most probable root causes.

2. *CAPA Plan.* This includes corrections, corrective actions, and preventive actions and the evaluation of their implementation and effectiveness

3. *Investigation Report and CAPA Assessment.* This form is recommended for the reviewer when documenting the merits of an investigation and/or CAPA plan. It is also recommended for the investigator when a self-assessment of the investigation is made.

4. *Human Error Investigation Form.* This form is recommended to be used when human error is the apparent causal factor of the event. The form allows discovery of a potential precursor or hidden human factors that can be associated with the situation under investigation.

7.1 EVENT DESCRIPTION AND INVESTIGATION

EVENT INFORMATION

Affected product/process/system: _____

Date occurred:_____

Date discovered: _____

Date reported: _____

_____

DESCRIPTION OF THE ISSUE

What happened? _____

What should have happened? (What is the specification, instruction, etc.)

_____

Where did it happen? _____

How was the event discovered? _____

When was it discovered? _____

Who discovered it? _____

_____

IMMEDIATE ACTIONS TAKEN

What has been done since discovering the event? _____

_____

_____

INITIAL IMPACT ASSESSMENT[1]

Does this situation impact other products, equipment, raw materials/
components, and/or systems?_____

_____

_____

[1] Use information described in Chapter 3.1.2

If product is involved in this event, identify and evaluate lots/batches that ran before and/or after the event under investigation. _____

Has any affected material already been released/distributed to customers?_____

Risk of the event: ☐ Low   ☐ Medium   ☐ High

INVESTIGATION DETAILS

Problem definition

- Background and historical data (trend analysis)
- Chronology of the event
- Comparison matrix (Is–Is Not)

Current Barrier Analysis

Root cause analysis

- Causal factors
- Potential root causes
  - Cause-and-effect diagram
  - Fault tree analysis

CONCLUSION ABOUT ROOT CAUSES

What is (are) the most probable root cause(s) of this event?

Root cause classification _____ Code_____

7.2 CAPA PLAN

CAPA PLAN

a. **Correction**/Containment actions taken

b. **Corrective Actions.** Must have at least one identified CA for each root cause already identified. Each corrective action must include the following information:

Corrective Action #1:

How will this action avoid the recurrence of the identified root cause?

_____

If the proposed CA is not immediate, provide interim actions. _____

_____

Implementation Verification:

How:_____

When:_____ Responsible: _____

Effectiveness Check:

How:_____

When:_____ Responsible: _____

Can this action be extended to another product/process/system not yet affected by this root cause? If yes, open a preventive action. _____

c. **Preventive Actions.** Should have at least one identified PA for each potential root cause already identified. Each preventive action must include the following information:

Preventive Action #1:

How will this action avoid the occurrence of the identified root cause?

_____

If the proposed PA is not immediate, provide interim actions:_____

_____

Implementation Verification:

How:_____

When:_____ Responsible: _____

Effectiveness Check:

How:_____

When:_____ Responsible: _____

7.3 INVESTIGATION REPORT AND CAPA ASSESSMENT FORM

Investigation Report No.	
Writer	
Reviewer	
Approved____ Rejected____	Date
Comments	

CRITERIA	YES	NO	COMMENTS
DESCRIPTION OF THE EVENT *Does the report clearly describe:*			
Affected product/process/system			
Date occurred			
Date discovered			
Date reported			
What happened			
What should have happened (the specification or instruction)			
Where it happened			
How the event was discovered			
When it was discovered			
Who discovered it			

CRITERIA	YES	NO	COMMENTS
IMMEDIATE ACTIONS TAKEN *Does the report clearly describe:*			
What has been done since discovering the event			
INITIAL IMPACT ASSESSMENT *Does the report clearly describe:*			
Does this situation impact other products, equipment, raw materials, components, and/or systems?			
If a product is involved in this event, the lots/batches that ran before and/or after the event under investigation.			
Whether any affected material has been already released/distributed to customers			
Risk of the event			

CRITERIA	YES	NO	COMMENTS
INVESTIGATION DETAILS *Does the report clearly describe:*			
Background and historical data (trend analysis)			
Chronology of the event			
Comparison matrix (Is–Is Not)			
Current barrier analysis			
Causal factors			
Potential root causes			
Cause-and-effect diagram			
Fault tree analysis			

CRITERIA	YES	NO	COMMENTS
CONCLUSION ABOUT ROOT CAUSES *Does the report clearly describe:*			
The most probable root causes of this event			
Root cause category			
CAPA PLAN – CORRECTION *Does the report clearly describe:*			
Correction/containment actions taken			
CAPA PLAN – CA *Does the report clearly describe:*			
At least one identified CA for each root cause already identified			
How this action will avoid the recurrence of the identified root cause			
Interim actions, if the proposed CA is not immediate			
Implementation verification: how, when, and by whom			
Effectiveness check: how, when, and by whom			
Whether this action can be extended to another product/process/system not yet affected by this root cause. If yes, was a preventive action opened?			

CRITERIA	YES	NO	COMMENTS
CAPA PLAN – PA *Does the report clearly describe:*			
At least one identified CA for each *potential* root cause already identified			
How this action will avoid the occurrence of the identified root cause?			
If the proposed PA is not immediate, provide any interim action(s)?			
Implementation verification: how, when, and by whom			
Effectiveness check: how, when, and by whom			
FINAL DISPOSITION/APPROVAL *Does the report clearly describe:*			
The final decision taken regarding the affected product/process/system			
Approval signatures			
EXECUTIVE SUMMARY *Does the report:*			
Provide a short summary of the investigation facts and results, from the description of the event to the list of correction, corrective actions, and preventive actions taken.			

CRITERIA	YES	NO	COMMENTS
OVERALL WRITING EFFECTIVENESS *Does the report:*			
Contain clear narrative (does it stands alone without the author "interpreting" it?)			
Contain concise narrative (to the point)			
Follow a logical flow (any educated reviewer or inspector can follow and understand it)			
Provide objective evidence to support conclusions			
Contain an impersonal "tone" without opinions, guessing, or passion? Only facts and objective data!			

7.4 HUMAN ERROR INVESTIGATION FORM

Table 7.1 contains 36 questions that can be used as guidance during the investigation of human errors. The purpose of these questions is to obtain a better understanding of the human factors surrounding the issue under investigation. It is not a mere checklist and it must be used along with regular root cause analysis tools such as cause-and-effect diagrams and fault tree analysis.

Table 7.1 Human error investigation form.

1. Is there a formal (written) instruction to perform this task?	☐ YES	☐ NO
2. Does the task require the employee to follow a specific sequence of steps?	☐ YES	☐ NO
3. Did the employee miss the task (omission error)?	☐ YES	☐ NO
4. Did the employee erroneously perform the task (commission error)?	☐ YES	☐ NO
5. Were procedures or working instructions available in the immediate area where the task was performed?	☐ YES	☐ NO
6. Did the employee read the procedure or work instruction while executing the task?	☐ YES	☐ NO
7. Did the employee work from memory while executing this task?	☐ YES	☐ NO
8. Was the employee formally trained on the task or procedure?	☐ YES	☐ NO
9. How was the employee trained on this task? (Describe the training method.)		
10. Does the training cover this specific task?	☐ YES	☐ NO
11. What was the length of the training for this specific task?		
12. What reason did the employee provide to justify this error? Explain.		
13. Review the procedure or working instruction with the employee and verify current practices against written instructions. Explain.		
14. Is the procedure or working instruction clear and well understood by the employee?	☐ YES	☐ NO
15. Does the procedure or working instruction have sufficient level of detail?	☐ YES	☐ NO
16. Did the procedure or working instruction use a qualitative description (slowly, soon, few, well, and so on) rather than specific details?	☐ YES	☐ NO
17. Can procedures or working instructions be considered adequate in terms of format, content, level of details, and so on? Explain.		
18. Does the employee clearly understand the applicable procedure or working instruction?	☐ YES	☐ NO

Continued

Table 7.1 Human error investigation form.	*Continued*

19. Was the employee working on "autopilot" because he/she is very familiar to the task?	☐ YES ☐ NO
20. Was the employee performing any other task concurrently?	☐ YES ☐ NO
21. Is this the first time the employee performed this task?	☐ YES ☐ NO
21.1 If it's not the first time, when was the last time he/she performed this task?	
21.2 If it's not the first time, how often does the employee perform this task?	
22. How many other employees do the same task correctly under the same conditions?	
23. Has the employee performed the task correctly earlier?	☐ YES ☐ NO
24. Who trained this employee?	
25. Who trained the other employees who did the task correctly?	
26. How often did this (or similar) error occur during the last year?	
27. Was the area's layout or workspace overcrowded?	☐ YES ☐ NO
28. Were working conditions comfortable (noise, temperature, humidity, illumination, and so on)?	☐ YES ☐ NO
29. Was the supervisor or group leader present when the error occurred?	☐ YES ☐ NO
30. Did the error occur during overtime?	☐ YES ☐ NO
31. When exactly did the error occur? (Be precise.)	
32. Did the error occur prior to or after a break or shift change?	☐ YES ☐ NO
33. Did the error occur prior to or after a shutdown or vacation period?	☐ YES ☐ NO
34. Was it a situation of competing priorities?	☐ YES ☐ NO
35. Was it a situation of very tight deadline?	☐ YES ☐ NO
36. Was it a situation of resource shortage?	☐ YES ☐ NO

8
CAPA Final Recommendations

Topics	Recommendations
Problem detection	• Use risk assessment criteria to prioritize your CAPA activities • Monitor in-conformance results • Consider all available sources of CAPA data
Problem investigation	• Do not use human error as root cause • Establish the requirements for using problem-solving tools (comparison diagram, timeline, fishbone, FTA, and so on).
Human error investigation	• Interview human beings involved with each incident • Investigate human factors • Look for precursor (latent) factors
CAPA plan	• One corrective action per each root cause • Do not use *evaluate, analyze,* or *assess* as corrective or preventive action • Do not abuse retraining
Effectiveness evaluation	• Do not use a fixed period of time • Link it to root cause, not symptoms
Management of the CAPA system	• Maintain only one CAPA system • Correlate systems, if using more than one (external, internal, and so on) • Develop your CAPA personnel

Continued

Topics	Recommendations
Documenting CAPA	• Clarity • Readability • Economy • Correctness
Training for CAPA	• Certify your CAPA personnel • Evaluate the effectiveness of your CAPA training

Human error prevention	• Eliminate the error source; make the error impossible by design
	• Do not allow personnel to operate by memory (read, execute, and document is the best recipe to prevent human errors)
	• Reduce the error opportunity using physical barriers
	• Mitigate the consequences of an error
	• Make the errors detectable before they create a greater problem
	• Reinforce supervision for new employees, tasks, or equipment)
	• Improve documents/work instructions:
	  – Employees without supervision must follow the procedures
	  – Provide reminders (warnings) when appropriate
	• Improve the effectiveness of the training

Appendix A

ADDITIONAL RESOURCES

Andersen, B. and T. Fagerhaug. 2006. *Root Cause Analysis: Simplified Tools and Techniques.* 2nd ed. Milwaukee, WI: ASQ Quality Press.

Gawande, A. 2010. *The Checklist Manifesto: How to Get Things Right.* New York, NY: Metropolitan Books.

Phillips, J. J. and R. D. Stone. 2002. *How to Measure Training Results: A Practical Guide to Tracking the Six Key Indicators.* New York, NY: McGraw-Hill.

Reason, J. and A. Hobbs. 2003. *Managing Maintenance Error: A Practical Guide.* Burlington, VT: Ashgate.

Wilson, P. F., L. D. Dell, and G. F. Anderson. 1993. *Root Cause Analysis: A Tool for Total Quality Management.* Milwaukee, WI: ASQ Quality Press.

USEFUL WEB SITES

http://ec.europa.eu/enterprise/sectors/pharmaceuticals/documents/ eudralex/index_en.htm

The body of European Union legislation in the pharmaceutical sector is compiled here.

http://www.asq.org

The American Society for Quality (ASQ) is the world's leading membership organization devoted to quality. This site provides useful information, resources, and links for quality topics.

http://www.fda.gov

This is the entry page to the U.S. Food and Drug Administration.

http://www.fda.gov/ora

This page contains significant ORA documents (consent decrees, 483 forms, Establishment Inspection Reports, and many more regulatory documents) under its ORA FOIA Electronic Reading Room.

http://www.fda.gov/ICECI/EnforcementActions/WarningLetters/default.htm

This is the place to see FDA published warning letters sent to regulated firms.

http://www.fda.gov/Safety/Recalls/default.htm

This section includes the most significant product actions over the last five years based on the extent of distribution and the degree of health risk. In this section, you will find a listing of FDA and industry press releases regarding product recalls. It includes a link to weekly FDA Enforcement Reports.

http://www.capapr.com

Author's web page devoted to the CAPA system and the regulated industry.

http://www.calidadpr.com

Author's page devoted to general quality topics (in Spanish).

http://www.ich.org

The International Conference on Harmonization of Technical Requirements for Registration of Pharmaceuticals for Human Use (ICH) is a unique project that brings together the regulatory authorities of Europe, Japan, and the United States and experts from the pharmaceutical industry in the three regions to discuss scientific and technical aspects of product registration.

http://www.ghtf.org

The Global Harmonization Task Force was conceived in 1992 in an effort to achieve greater uniformity between national medical device regulatory systems. A partnership between regulatory authorities and regulated industry, the GHTF, is made up of five founding members: European Union, United States, Canada, Australia, and Japan.

Acronyms

CAPA	Corrective and preventive action
CDER	FDA's Center for Drug Evaluation and Research
CDRH	FDA's Center for Devices and Radiological Health
CFR	Code of Federal Regulations
CGMP	Current good manufacturing practice
FDA	Food and Drug Administration
FMEA	Failure modes and effects analysis
FTA	Fault tree analysis
GHTF	Global Harmonization Task Force
ICH	International Conference on Harmonization
ISO	International Standardization Organization
OOC	Out of control
OOS	Out of specification
OOT	Out of trend
ORA	FDA's Office of Regulatory Affairs
QMS	Quality management system
QSIT	FDA's quality system inspection technique
QSR	FDA's quality system regulations
RCA	Root cause analysis

Glossary

adverse trend: A general drift or tendency in a set of data to exceed established limits over an established period of time.

action threshold: A statistical limit based on historical data used to indicate an adverse trend, requiring an action. See OOC.

annual review: An evaluation, conducted at least annually, that assesses the quality standards of each drug product to determine the need for changes in the drug product specifications or manufacturing or control procedures.

CAPA (corrective and preventive action): A systematic approach that includes actions needed to correct ("correction"), avoid recurrence ("corrective action"), and eliminate the cause of potential nonconforming product and other quality problems (preventive action).

CAPA plan: Encompasses the identification of corrective and/or preventive actions, their verification and/or validation (prior to implementation), their implementation, and finally the evaluation of the plan's effectiveness.

causal factor: Any failure (human, equipment, or material/component) that directly caused the incident, allowed it to occur, or allowed the consequence to be worse.

concession: A special approval granted to release a nonconforming product for use or delivery. Concessions are usually limited by time and quantity and tend to specify that nonconforming characteristics may not violate specified limits.

continuous improvement: Ongoing activities to evaluate and positively change products, processes, and the quality system to increase effectiveness.

control limit (CL): A horizontal line on a control chart that represents a boundary for a process. If the process strays beyond a control limit, it may be out of control.

correction: Action to eliminate a detected nonconformity. Corrections typically are one-time fixes. A correction is an immediate solution such as repair or rework. Also known as remedial or containment action.

corrective action: Action to eliminate the causes of a detected nonconformity or other undesirable situation. The corrective action should eliminate the recurrence of the issue.[1]

customer: A person or organization (internal or external) that receives a product or service anywhere along the product's life cycle.

discrepancy: Datum or result outside of the expected range; an unfulfilled requirement. May be called nonconformity, defect, deviation, out of specification, out of limit, out of trend.

effectiveness: The degree to which a planned effect is achieved. Planned activities are effective if these activities are realized. Similarly, planned results are effective if these results are actually achieved. For example, an effective process is one that realizes planned activities and achieves planned results. Similarly, an effective set of characteristics or specifications is one that has the potential to realize planned activities and achieve planned results.

effectiveness evaluation: documented process to establish that an action was effective and accomplished the objective that was intended.

efficiency: A relationship between results achieved (outputs) and resources used (inputs). Efficiency can be enhanced by achieving more with the same or fewer resources. The efficiency of a process or system can be enhanced by achieving more or getting better results (outputs) with the same or fewer resources (inputs).

current good manufacturing practices (CGMP): A set of current regulations for the control and management of manufacturing and quality control of foods, pharmaceutical products, and medical devices. GMPs are guidelines that outline the aspects of production that would affect the quality of a product. Many countries have created their own GMP guidelines that correspond with their legislation.

harm: Damage to health, including damage that can occur from the loss of product quality or availability (ICH Q9). Physical injury or damage to health of people or damage to property or the environment (ANSI/AAMI/ISO 14971:2007, ISO/IEC Guide 51:1999).

---

[1] ANSI/ISO/ASQ Q9001-2008 section 8.5.2 defines corrective action as "action to eliminate the causes of nonconformities in order to prevent recurrence."

investigation: Thorough, timely, unbiased, well-documented, and scientifically sound process used to discover the root causes of the problem.

metric: A quantitative measurement that is collected, recorded, and analyzed to determine whether quality system goals and objectives have been met or exceeded or failed to meet the requirements.

monitor: To observe and check over a period of time; to maintain regular close observation over a process.

nonconformance: Non-fulfillment of specified requirements.

nonconformity: A deficiency in a characteristic, product specification, process parameter, record, or procedure that renders the quality of a product unacceptable, indeterminate, or not according to specified requirements.

objective evidence: Data that show or prove that something exists or is true. Objective evidence can be collected by means of observations, measurements, tests, or any other suitable method.

out of control (OOC): Any data points outside of control chart limits that represent the natural boundaries of the process.

out of specification (OOS): Test results (in-process and final) that fall outside the established specifications or acceptance criteria.

preventive action: Action to eliminate the cause of a potential nonconformity or other undesirable potential situation. The preventive action should prevent the occurrence of the potential issue.

product/service: The intended results of activities or processes; products/services can be tangible or intangible.

quality: The degree to which a set of inherent characteristics fulfills requirements. A measure of a product's or service's ability to satisfy the customer's stated or implied needs.

quality assurance: Proactive and retrospective activities that provide confidence that requirements are fulfilled.

quality control: The steps taken during the generation of a product or service to ensure that it meets requirements and that the product or service is reproducible.

quality management: Coordinated activities to direct and control an organization with regard to quality.

quality management system (QMS): Management system to direct and control an organization with regard to quality.

quality objectives: Specific measurable activities or processes to meet the intentions and directions as defined in the quality policy.

quality plan: The documented result of quality planning that is disseminated to all relevant levels of the organization.

quality planning: A management activity that sets quality objectives and defines the operational and/or quality system processes and the resources needed to fulfill the objectives.

quality policy: A statement of intentions and direction issued by the highest level of the organization related to satisfying customer needs. It is similar to a strategic direction that communicates quality expectations that the organization is striving to achieve.

quality system: Formalized business practices that define management responsibilities for organizational structure, processes, procedures, and resources needed to fulfill product/service requirements, customer satisfaction, and continuous improvement.

quality system degulations (QSR): U.S. medical devices regulations (Title 21 CFR §820).

requirement: Need or expectation that is stated, generally implied or obligatory.

rework: Action taken on a nonconforming product so that it will fulfill the specified requirements before it is released for distribution.

risk: The combination of the probability of occurrence of harm and the severity of that harm.

risk assessment: A systematic process for organizing information to support a risk decision that is made within a risk management process. The process consists of the identification of hazards and the analysis and evaluation of risks associated with exposure to those hazards.

risk management: The systematic application of quality management policies, procedures, and practices to the tasks of assessing, controlling, communicating, and reviewing risk.

root cause: A gap in a process input or supporting business system that is, at least partly, responsible for the incident. It is the basic reasons why causal factors occur and/or persist.

root cause analysis (RCA): Analysis necessary to determine the original or true cause of a system, product, or process nonconformity. This effort extends beyond the effects of a problem to discover its most fundamental cause.

specification: Any requirement with which a product, process, service, or other activity must conform.

stakeholder: An individual or organization having an ownership or interest in the delivery, results, and metrics of the quality system framework or business process improvements.

trend: A sequence or pattern of data. Analysis of a trend is performed to detect a special cause amidst the random variation of data.

timeliness: A timeframe commensurate with the risk and magnitude of the issue; considered reasonable by a company that is concerned with protecting the public health.

validation: Confirmation, through the provision of objective evidence, that the requirements for a specific intended use or application can be consistently fulfilled.

verification: Confirmation, through the provision of objective evidence, that specified requirements have been fulfilled.

Bibliography

Ammerman, M. 1998. *The Root Cause Analysis Handbook: A Simplified Approach to Identifying, Correcting, and Reporting Workplace Errors.* New York: Productivity Press.

Daniel, A. and E. Kimmelman. 2008. *The FDA and Worldwide Quality System Regulations Guidebook for Medical Devices.* 2nd ed. Milwaukee, WI: ASQ Quality Press.

Dekker, S. 2006. *The Field Guide to Understanding Human Error.* Burlington, VT: Ashgate.

European Pharmaceutical GMP. *EudraLex* Volume 4 (2003). The body of European Union legislation in the pharmaceutical sector is compiled in Volume 1 and Volume 5 of the publication "The rules governing medicinal products in the European Union." It can be downloaded from: http://ec.europa.eu/enterprise/sectors/pharmaceuticals/documents/eudralex/index_en.htm

FDA. *21 Code of Federal Regulations §Part 210: Current manufacturing practice in manufacturing, processing, packing, or holding of drugs; general* (1978). Can be downloaded from: http://www.accessdata.fda.gov/scripts/cdrh/cfdocs/cfcfr/CFRSearch.cfm?CFRPart=210

FDA. *21 Code of Federal Regulations §Part 211: Current manufacturing practice for finished pharmaceuticals* (1978). Can be downloaded from: http://www.accessdata.fda.gov/scripts/cdrh/cfdocs/cfcfr/CFRSearch.cfm?CFRPart=211

Preamble of finished pharmaceuticals can be downloaded from: http://www.fda.gov/downloads/AboutFDA/CentersOffices/CDER/UCM095852.txt

FDA. *21 Code of Federal Regulation §Part 820: Medical Devices: Current Good Manufacturing Practice (CGMP) Final Rule: Quality System Regulations* (1996). Can be downloaded from: http://www.accessdata.fda.gov/scripts/cdrh/cfdocs/cfcfr/CFRSearch.cfm?CFRPart=820
Preamble of Medical Device Quality System Regulations can be downloaded from http://www.fda.gov/downloads/MedicalDevices/DeviceRegulationandGuidance/PostmarketRequirements/QualitySystems Regulations/MedicalDeviceQualitySystemsManual/UCM122806.pdf

FDA. *Guide to Inspections of Quality Systems* (1999). This guide can be downloaded from: www.fda.gov/downloads/ICECI/Inspections/UCM142981.pdf

FDA. *Guidance for Industry. Investigating Out-of-Specification (OOS) Test Results for Pharmaceutical Production* (2006).
Note: All FDA guidances can be downloaded from: http://www.fda.gov/regulatoryinformation/guidances/default.htm

FDA. *Guidance Do It By Design—An Introduction to Human Factors in Medical Devices* (1996).

FDA. *General Principles of Software Validation: Final Guidance for Industry and FDA Staff* (2002).

FDA. *Guidance for Industry: Quality Systems Approach to Pharmaceutical Current Good Manufacturing Practice Regulations* (2006).

FDA. *Guidance for Industry Sterile Drug Products Produced by Aseptic Processing— Current Good Manufacturing Practice* (2004).

Global Harmonization Task Force. SG 3 (PD)/N18R8: Quality management system—Medical Devices—Guidance on corrective action and preventive action and related QMS processes (2009). This guidance can be downloaded from: http://www.ghtf.org/sg3/sg3-proposed.html

International Standard, ISO 13485:2003 *Medical devices—Quality management systems— Requirements for regulatory purposes.*

International Standard, ISO/TR 14969: 2004 *Medical devices—Quality management systems—Guidance on the application of ISO 13485:2003.*

Kirkpatrick, D. L. and J. D. Kirkpatrick. 2006. *Evaluating Training Programs.* 3rd ed. San Francisco, CA: Berrett-Koehler Publishers.

Kirkpatrick, D. L. and J. D. Kirkpatrick. 2007. *Implementing the Four Levels: A Practical Guide for Effective Evaluation of Training Programs.* San Francisco, CA: Berrett-Koehler Publishers.

Kohn, L. T., J. M. Corrigan, and M. S. Donaldson, eds. *To Err is Human: Building a Safer Health System*. Washington, D.C.: Institute of Medicine Committee on Quality of Health Care in America.

Okes, D. 2009. *Root Cause Analysis: The Core of Problem Solving and Corrective Action*. Milwaukee, WI: ASQ Quality Press.

Reason, J. 1990. *Human Error*. New York: Cambridge University Press.

Reason, J. 2000. *Human Error: Models and Management*. BMJ 2000;320: 768–70.

Tague, N.R. 2005. *The Quality Toolbox*. 2nd ed. Milwaukee, WI: ASQ Quality Press.

Swain, A. D. and H. E. Guttman. 1983. *Handbook of Human Reliability Analysis with Emphasis on Nuclear Power Plant Applications*. NUREG/CR 1278. Albuquerque, NM: Sandia National Laboratories.

Index

Page numbers in *italics* refer to tables or illustrations.

Belong to the Quality Community!

Established in 1946, ASQ is a global community of quality experts in all fields and industries. ASQ is dedicated to the promotion and advancement of quality tools, principles, and practices in the workplace and in the community.

The Society also serves as an advocate for quality. Its members have informed and advised the U.S. Congress, government agencies, state legislatures, and other groups and individuals worldwide on quality-related topics.

Vision

By making quality a global priority, an organizational imperative, and a personal ethic, ASQ becomes the community of choice for everyone who seeks quality technology, concepts, or tools to improve themselves and their world.

ASQ is...

- More than 90,000 individuals and 700 companies in more than 100 countries

- The world's largest organization dedicated to promoting quality

- A community of professionals striving to bring quality to their work and their lives

- The administrator of the Malcolm Baldrige National Quality Award

- A supporter of quality in all sectors including manufacturing, service, healthcare, government, and education

- YOU

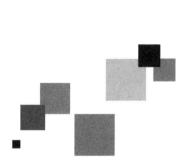

Visit www.asq.org for more information.

ASQ Membership

Research shows that people who join associations experience increased job satisfaction, earn more, and are generally happier.* ASQ membership can help you achieve this while providing the tools you need to be successful in your industry and to distinguish yourself from your competition. So why wouldn't you want to be a part of ASQ?

Networking

Have the opportunity to meet, communicate, and collaborate with your peers within the quality community through conferences and local ASQ section meetings, ASQ forums or divisions, ASQ Communities of Quality discussion boards, and more.

Professional Development

Access a wide variety of professional development tools such as books, training, and certifications at a discounted price. Also, ASQ certifications and the ASQ Career Center help enhance your quality knowledge and take your career to the next level.

Solutions

Find answers to all your quality problems, big and small, with ASQ's Knowledge Center, mentoring program, various e-newsletters, *Quality Progress* magazine, and industry-specific products.

Access to Information

Learn classic and current quality principles and theories in ASQ's Quality Information Center (QIC), *ASQ Weekly* e-newsletter, and product offerings.

Advocacy Programs

ASQ helps create a better community, government, and world through initiatives that include social responsibility, Washington advocacy, and Community Good Works.

Visit www.asq.org/membership for more information on ASQ membership.

*2008, The William E. Smith Institute for Association Research

ASQ Certification

ASQ certification is formal recognition by ASQ that an individual has demonstrated a proficiency within, and comprehension of, a specified body of knowledge at a point in time. Nearly 150,000 certifications have been issued. ASQ has members in more than 100 countries, in all industries, and in all cultures. ASQ certification is internationally accepted and recognized.

Benefits to the Individual

- New skills gained and proficiency upgraded
- Investment in your career
- Mark of technical excellence
- Assurance that you are current with emerging technologies
- Discriminator in the marketplace
- Certified professionals earn more than their uncertified counterparts
- Certification is endorsed by more than 125 companies

Benefits to the Organization

- Investment in the company's future
- Certified individuals can perfect and share new techniques in the workplace
- Certified staff are knowledgeable and able to assure product and service quality

Quality is a global concept. It spans borders, cultures, and languages. No matter what country your customers live in or what language they speak, they demand quality products and services. You and your organization also benefit from quality tools and practices. Acquire the knowledge to position yourself and your organization ahead of your competition.

Certifications Include

- Biomedical Auditor – CBA
- Calibration Technician – CCT
- HACCP Auditor – CHA
- Pharmaceutical GMP Professional – CPGP
- Quality Inspector – CQI
- Quality Auditor – CQA
- Quality Engineer – CQE
- Quality Improvement Associate – CQIA
- Quality Technician – CQT
- Quality Process Analyst – CQPA
- Reliability Engineer – CRE
- Six Sigma Black Belt – CSSBB
- Six Sigma Green Belt – CSSGB
- Software Quality Engineer – CSQE
- Manager of Quality/Organizational Excellence – CMQ/OE

Visit www.asq.org/certification to apply today!

ASQ Training

Classroom-based Training

ASQ offers training in a traditional classroom setting on a variety of topics. Our instructors are quality experts and lead courses that range from one day to four weeks, in several different cities. Classroom-based training is designed to improve quality and your organization's bottom line. Benefit from quality experts; from comprehensive, cutting-edge information; and from peers eager to share their experiences.

Web-based Training

Virtual Courses

ASQ's virtual courses provide the same expert instructors, course materials, interaction with other students, and ability to earn CEUs and RUs as our classroom-based training, without the hassle and expenses of travel. Learn in the comfort of your own home or workplace. All you need is a computer with Internet access and a telephone.

Self-paced Online Programs

These online programs allow you to work at your own pace while obtaining the quality knowledge you need. Access them whenever it is convenient for you, accommodating your schedule.

Some Training Topics Include

- Auditing
- Basic Quality
- Engineering
- Education
- Healthcare
- Government
- Food Safety
- ISO
- Leadership
- Lean
- Quality Management
- Reliability
- Six Sigma
- Social Responsibility

Visit www.asq.org/training for more information.